Navigating the Politics of UX

More Strategies and Stories
from 40 Years in the Trenches

Research Obstacles

Inspiring Colleagues

Driving Innovation

Leadership Challenges

Leading Your Team

Managing Your Career

What's Next for UX?

Volume 2: Challenges

John Scott Bowie

Navigating the Politics of UX: More Strategies and Stories from 40 Years in the Trenches, Volume 2: Challenges

Publisher: Colorado Design Labs LLC Loveland, CO 80538

Author: John Scott Bowie

Library of Congress Control Number: 2025920452

ISBN: 979-8-9851752-3-3

ISBN: 979-8-9851752-4-0 (ebook)

DEDICATION

This book is dedicated to all the user experience professionals with whom I've had the honor to work over the past forty years. From you I have learned everything I know.

Keep up your good and important work.

And never stop asking "What's Next?"

ACKNOWLEDGMENTS

Thanks to Giselle Daniela Vázquez Chan, Timothy Chan, Carlos Martínez Domínguez, Vivian Gomes, Ariel Grace Snapp, Chuck Griffith, Jacqui Miller, Zack Naylor, Karthikeyan Panneerselvam, Scott Parker, Jigar Tewar, and James Young for generously donating their stories and expertise to Chapter 7.

Contents

x

Foreword: Why I *Almost* Changed the Title

My first book was called *Navigating the Politics of UX*. For this second book in the series, I considered changing the title to *Navigating the Politics of UX and Product Design*.

Why did I consider it? If you scan job boards today, you'll find two categories of openings—roles for UX Designers and roles for Product Designers.

To me, however, experience design and product design are not separate disciplines. They are two sides of the same coin. You can't design a product without simultaneously designing the experience of using it.

Early in my career, I came to the realization that when you design a product, you also design its user. Every function in a product comes with an implicit expectation that the human user can and will find and correctly operate that function. In other words, the product requires its human user to have complementary functionality "installed" in their brains to successfully interact with it.

The product's functionality can be coded, tested, and delivered relatively bug-free. But the human user? Their functional "requirements" are less predictable. The human functionality required to operate the product is often absent and must be "uploaded" through training sessions, support sites, or 300-page manuals.

That is what makes UX design so challenging. Technology has fixed performance characteristics. People do not. The way you assign functional responsibility to humans must account for high variability, limiting constraints, and the reality that most people do not want to become product superusers just to get their work done.

Several decades ago, engineers believed products could be designed independently of users. The burden was on humans to adapt to machines. They expected anyone who used their products to read the manual, master the technical terminology, and understand the product's underlying mechanics.

During this era, one of my first documentation projects was writing a computer workstation's "Operating Manual" in which I attempted to educate users on setting RAM starting addresses, choosing select codes for interfaces, and configuring UNIX to recognize attached peripherals like printers and plotters.

Today, we are more enlightened (?). We know products must not only be functional but also usable. We recognize that people do not buy technology to learn technology. They buy it to achieve outcomes.

This is why UX design and product design are inseparable. Together they produce products and services that collaborate with humans to achieve promised outcomes with as little friction as possible.

So, don't get hung up debating terminology. Whatever your job title—UX designer, product designer, product manager, product owner, or service designer—if your job is to ensure products and people succeed together, then I am writing the *Navigating the Politics of UX* series for you.

Rather than distinguishing experience design from product design as two separate disciplines, think of them as having a common goal: to build *human-product systems* for achieving outcomes and results. My goal is to help you navigate the politics of this role so that your ideas are implemented, your influence grows, your customers and your company are happy, and your career continues to evolve and advance.

Chapter 1: Research Obstacles

I've often said that research is the solution to everything. Not because it answers every question, but because it forces us to ask the *right* ones. Yet, in so many companies I've worked with, research has been the first thing to get cut: underfunded, understaffed, or dismissed altogether.

Over the years, I've experienced the full spectrum of user research support. At one extreme were organizations that gave me unlimited access to customers with a virtually unlimited travel budget. At the other extreme were those that treated research as an unnecessary indulgence and an impediment to release schedules. Somewhere in between were companies that wanted the benefits of insight but weren't willing to slow down long enough to earn it.

With all the evidence showing that user research has an incredibly high ROI, there are still teams who believe they know everything about their users because, in their minds, they *are* the user.

In this chapter, I share some of the battles I've fought to make research matter: the small wins that opened leadership's eyes, the pushback that revealed deeper cultural barriers, and the breakthroughs that transformed a company's culture. Each story is a reminder that research is the engine of innovation and the truest measure of UX maturity.

Flipping the Script on User Requirements
Where is the *Real* Performance Problem?

Early in my career, I was the lone user advocate in a company dominated by engineers. The organization spoke the language of

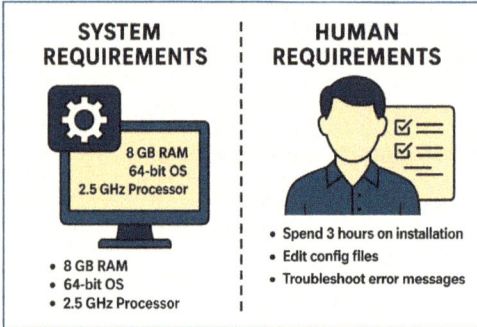

throughput, benchmarks, and processor speed. My language was about pain points, usability, and why product complexity impeded customer success. I had to find a way to express human-centered design in engineering terms.

One of my first attempts occurred when I was given a few minutes with a vice president to pitch a UX initiative I wanted to pursue. I asked him to describe his top three priorities for the coming year, hoping that ease of use or increasing customer productivity might be among them. But he replied without hesitation: "My top three priorities? Performance. Performance. Performance."

He was talking about processor speed as measured in millions of instructions per second (MIPS), an industry benchmark against which all computer workstations were measured. I tried to tell him the real throughput bottleneck wasn't in our machines, but in the time it took our users to install, configure, and troubleshoot our computers. But it was clear that argument gained no traction with him.

To change this singular focus on product performance held by engineers, I offered workshops that redefined the meaning of "user requirements." Our product teams defined user requirements as the requirements our customers expected from our products. I reversed the meaning, defining user requirements as the technical knowledge our products demanded from our customers.

At that time, software came in a box. Clearly stated on the packaging was a list of "System Requirements:" processor speed, operating system version, minimum memory required, disk space needed for installation, etc.

So, I created an example of a "Human Requirements" panel that we should print on our product's box if we were going to be honest about the demands we expected from our users:

- Must spend two hours installing the product.
- Must be comfortable editing configuration files without clear instructions.
- Must be able to troubleshoot vague error messages by trial and error.
- Must read our 300-page user manual from cover to cover before use.

And so on.

I dramatized this point by telling a story. I was working in my home office one day when my son poked his head through the door. He was trying to install a new video game on our computer, but before he could do so, the game asked him to provide the DMA channel of our sound card, along with the IRQ and I/O Base Address. My son—a child!—was *required by the product* to supply this information as a prerequisite to playing the game.

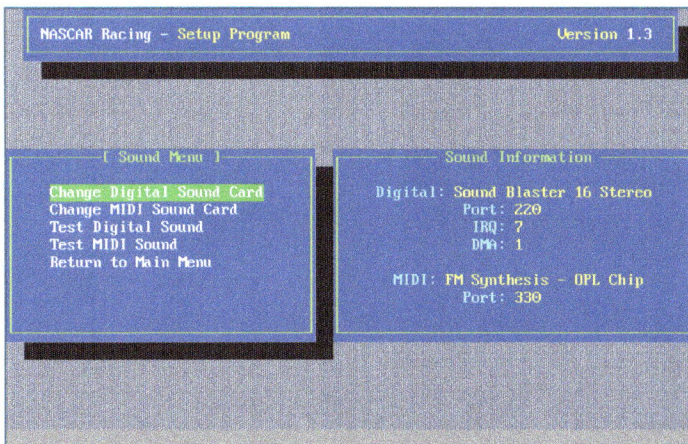

After 45 minutes of searching through documentation, fiddling with hardware, and rebooting my computer several times, I finally found the requisite information and finished the installation.

The video game box contained no Human Requirements panel. There was no warning stating that users must first find and deliver the DMA channel, IRQ, and I/O Base Address of the computer's sound card before they could achieve the desired outcome of playing a game.

But it should have. Either that or the product team should have redesigned the installation process to remove these requirements from the user experience. But product teams are often so familiar with their foundational technology that they fail to perceive the technical requirements they impose upon their users. (See the next story about the Smart People Paradox.)

The Lesson: Express Usability in Engineering Terms

Products can't achieve outcomes by themselves. Human beings must be able to complete the tasks the product assigns to them. If the requirements the product delegates to the human being can't be easily performed, the outcome will not be achieved—just as certainly as when the product contains critical bugs and crashes. Designing only the product and ignoring the human side of the design is a recipe for failure.

Engineers often do not have this mindset. Reframing user requirements as the burdens the product imposes on people helps our colleagues see the hidden costs of complexity. To back up your claims, you must include developers in user research where they can see firsthand the frustration customers face as a result of carelessly assigning technical requirements to users.

Only then will they fully appreciate your repeated appeals to consider the human impact of their design decisions.

Call to Action: Define User *and* Product Requirements

Change the conversation at your next user requirements meeting. The next time you gather with your product team to define user requirements for an upcoming release, ask whether you can have five minutes to suggest a new approach you've learned.

I led a success workshop in these situations to precisely define what success looks like—for our product, for our company, for us as individuals, and, most importantly, for our customers. Without going into the details here, you basically reach agreement that you, your product, and your company can't succeed unless your customers do. Your viability as a company is dependent upon the ability of customers to achieve the outcomes and results you promised them—without frustration and expending unreasonable effort.

Once you reach agreement on this point, reframe defining requirements as a two-part exercise:

1. Defining the outcomes customers require of your product, and,
2. Defining what your product requires of your customers in order to achieve those outcomes.

Express both requirements as companion user stories:

- As a <user>, I can use this product to achieve <outcome> so that I can receive < benefit>.
- As a <product>, I expect my <user> to be able to perform < actions> and know or find <information> so that the <outcome> can be achieved.

This pair of complementary stories defines the requirements the user has for the product, and the requirements the product has for the user. Both requirements must be met; otherwise, the human-product system fails.

"We Already Know What Our Users Want"
Exposing the Smart People Paradox

One of the most persistent challenges I've encountered in product design is what I call the Smart People Paradox. Companies hire brilliant subject matter experts (SMEs) to build technically complex products. Yet those same experts often assume that users are just like them: equally knowledgeable, equally immersed in the domain, and equally comfortable navigating complexity. As a result, products are built by and for experts. But most users are *not* experts, nor do they want to be; they are simply people with a job to do.

I first ran into this paradox early in my career as a technical writer. I had just completed a draft of a user guide when a senior colleague pulled me aside. "Let's rewrite this on a college level," he exclaimed, unimpressed with my effort. To him, writing was an opportunity to display the author's intelligence, to impress rather than to inform. He was more concerned with sounding smart to his readers than with expressing complex technology in simple terms.

I took his advice and revised the section accordingly. When I handed it off to my manager for review, he flipped through it, looked up, and said bluntly, "This is gobbledygook." It was the best feedback I ever received.

The company was heavily engineering-driven. The prevailing belief was that since our products were designed *for* scientists and engineers *by* scientists and engineers, they would naturally be comfortable with complexity. The mantra was, "Sure, our products are complex, but they're not rocket science."

That assumption fell apart when I accompanied several engineers to Los Alamos National Laboratory where many of our users were actual rocket scientists. They told us our products were hard to use. They said they no longer had time to read manuals or wrestle with unintuitive interfaces. They had more important jobs to do than spend hours learning to use our products.

That was an epiphany for many of our product managers and engineers. For the first time, they realized that documenting complexity was not enough. Even our scientist/engineer customers wanted and expected a simple user experience.

The Lesson: Introduce SMEs to Customers

Simplifying a product's user experience is *not* "dumbing it down." It is respecting users' time, attention, and priorities. People buy products to achieve results quickly and easily. No one wants to spend hours deciphering a manual just to get work done.

The best way to broaden SMEs' understanding is to expose them to real customers. Seeing how people actually use products and where they struggle forces a shift in perspective. This direct exposure helps experts appreciate that users are not like them.

Call to Action: Help SMEs See What Customers See

Expose SMEs to research. Invite them to usability tests or on-site visits. Some will deflect blame, others may feel embarrassed, but either reaction can spark problem-solving. Ask: "If our customers feel this way, how could we simplify to meet their needs?"

Convince SMEs that not all smart people think like them. Record customers interacting with your product. Pay homage to your company SMEs' expertise while reinforcing that customer SMEs have different but equally important skillsets and priorities.

Use history as proof. Provide examples of how once-complex technologies evolved into mainstream products through simplification. Emphasize how reducing complexity expands markets and is a challenge worthy of their SME intelligence.

Nurturing a Partnership with Product Management
Celebrate Diversity of Perspectives

There is a fundamental difference between market research and UX research. It isn't only about methods or metrics; it's about mindset.

Complementary Perspectives on User Research

Patterns — Empathy

Product Management   UX Design

I worked for a VP who managed product management, engineering, and UX. This unusual structure meant we attended the same team meetings, discussed the same issues, and got to know our colleagues in the other functions as friends. Although we collaborated closely to make each new release succeed, it became clear how differently we viewed the world.

At one offsite for all the functional managers, a consultant administered a personality assessment and had us line up based on our scores. The people who received the most extreme scores were on each end and everyone else was in between. I stood at one end; the product management director stood at the other.

In some companies, differences like this create tension. In ours, the diversity in our personalities engendered fresh approaches to business problems that neither one of us could have come up with on our own.

When we traveled together to customer sites and compared our observations, we noticed different things. These differences allowed us to see customers from complementary angles. She focused on patterns in the market, while I focused on patterns of user behavior. She emphasized the "what" and "when" while I emphasized the "why" and "how." Together, we built a shared view that was richer than either of us could have created alone.

The Lesson: Value Tension Between Product and UX

Product management and UX design are fundamentally different disciplines, each requiring distinct skills and ways of thinking. When these differences are respected, collaboration produces better results than either role could achieve alone. But that kind of partnership does not happen automatically.

Too often, product managers and UX professionals see each other as rivals, especially when it comes to research. Sometimes product managers believe that control of customer access belongs exclusively to them. This doesn't need to create conflict. Product managers can take the lead on arranging customer visits, provided they are willing to invite UX into the conversation and share ownership of discovery.

The key is mutual trust and shared purpose. When both roles recognize the value the other brings to understanding customer needs, they move past rivalry and toward partnership. That shift makes all the difference in capturing a 360° view of your customers and the market.

Call to Action: Strengthen Your Partnerships

Join customer visits. Make it clear that you want to accompany product managers on customer calls or site visits. Let them observe how *your* questions complement *theirs* and produce a more complete understanding of customer needs and frustrations.

Debrief immediately. After each visit, share key takeaways. Discuss how small design changes could improve customer satisfaction and retention. Offer to prototype concepts that address customer concerns.

Suggest follow-ups. Propose returning to the same customer to validate insights and test early prototypes. These visits demonstrate your commitment to acting on customer suggestions and show how feedback shapes product decisions.

Growing a Nascent Research Practice
No Budget, No Problem

When I became the first UX director at a company with no existing practice, my first step was establishing a UX research program. There was no research team, no tools, no usability testing program, and no budget to create one. If I wanted to understand our customers and improve the user experience, I had to start with what was already available.

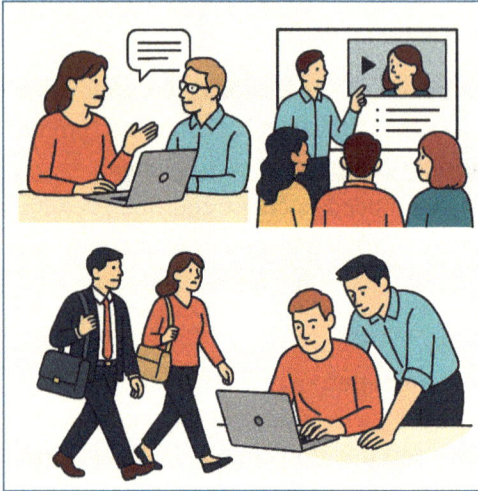

I began with simple, low-cost approaches. I visited local customers and asked for feedback on early design concepts. I went into retail stores where our products were sold and, with permission, talked to associates and customers.

I organized virtual advisory sessions and offered digital gift cards as small tokens of thanks. I sat quietly on sales calls to hear how customers described their challenges. I attended new customer training sessions and asked for five minutes at the end to collect feedback. I also partnered with product management to add a few UX-focused questions to their annual customer satisfaction survey, including an option for customers to volunteer for follow-up interviews. Support teams allowed me to listen in on calls, and occasionally I was able to ask clarifying questions at the close of a conversation.

As I shared the pain points, unmet needs, and emerging behavior patterns I identified, I also created quick design mockups to illustrate possible improvements. That visible connection between user insights and tangible solutions caught the attention of product managers, engineers, and even senior leaders. They began to see how direct user input could reduce rework, lower support costs, and make products easier to sell.

Eventually, this growing interest led to funding for tools, travel, and structured research. But the real win was not the budget. It was the credibility I achieved from these small customer interactions that demonstrated the value of research.

The Lesson: Starting Small Can Lead to Big Change

Choosing not to conduct research is not an option. Even with limited resources, you must create a foundation on which to build. Share what you learn, make it visible, and invite others into the process. When insights are tied to real outcomes, research stops being a UX-only activity, and becomes an essential part of product development.

Call to Action: Start with Low-Cost Research

Work with product managers to coordinate research. Always work closely with product managers to ensure they are aware of your efforts. Emphasize that your UX research program is an extension of their customer engagement initiatives.

Make a list of existing customer touchpoints. Consider local customers, retail outlets, sales calls, customer training sessions, call centers, responses to customer complaints, feedback channels, customer satisfaction surveys, social media—any time a customer interacts with your company.

Touch all the touchpoints. Find out who manages each touchpoint and ask how you can support their efforts and learn from them. Always share your findings.

Show research highlights monthly. Host short "movie" sessions featuring clips from interviews, usability tests, or field observations. Facilitate discussions afterward to spark ideas for improvement. Prototype solutions.

Conference Research
Testing Users in the Wild

Industry conferences are crowded, noisy, and often chaotic. They are also one of the most underused opportunities for targeted user research with customers and non-customers alike. With planning

and coordination, they can become powerful venues for usability testing, product validation, and brand building.

At one event, our team worked with the event organizers to secure a small private room near the main expo floor. Before the conference, we invited attendees to sign up for a 15-minute usability session. We offered gift cards as incentives.

Inside the quiet room, we ran task-based usability tests on potential solutions to known pain points. At the same time on the expo floor, we invited visitors to our booth to observe a five-minute demo session using a high-fidelity prototype of a new feature concept. These short demos provided quick feedback on the usability and appeal of a future product enhancement we were considering.

The diversity of participants revealed perspectives we rarely captured through traditional channels. We learned not only how *our* customers reacted, but also how customers of competing products viewed our concepts. This broadened our understanding of the market and gave us a chance to make positive impressions with people we might never have reached otherwise.

The benefits extended beyond UX. Sales gained qualified leads, product teams received fresh input, and marketing secured powerful customer stories. One of the concepts we tested went on to win "Best in Show" at the event, an award that elevated the role of UX and convinced company leadership that the contributions of research can strengthen our reputation as an industry leader.

The Lesson: Conferences Are a Valuable Research Venue

Industry events provide access to diverse users in a short period of time. They allow you to test ideas, capture quick reactions, and collect candid feedback. They also showcase the UX team's value to internal stakeholders while strengthening cross-functional collaboration. When used strategically, conferences can be more than marketing opportunities; they can be living laboratories for testing new design concepts.

Call to Action: Make Conferences Part of Research

Volunteer to work shifts at your company's booth. Trade your training budget for conference attendance if necessary. Use the opportunity to observe reactions to your products, listen to feedback, and ask follow-up questions.

Capture short video testimonials. When participants show enthusiasm, ask to record a brief statement. With permission, these clips become compelling evidence for internal storytelling.

Offer small incentives for participation. A modest gift card encourages attendees to spend a few minutes in a usability session and shows respect for their time.

Create quiet testing spaces. Secure a private room or use a nearby hotel suite to reduce distractions and gather higher-quality data.

Treat the expo floor as a lab. Use quick demos of high-fidelity prototypes to gather directional input from a wide range of people, including competitors' customers.

Engaging the Whole Organization in Usability Tests
Usability Watch Parties

At one point in my career, we decided to transform usability testing from something hidden behind closed doors into a

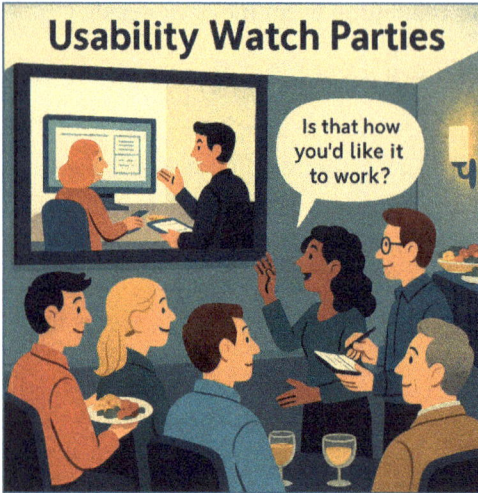

company-wide, social event. We partnered with a local marketing agency that had a classic usability lab setup: a testing room, a one-way mirror, and an observation space with plenty of seating.

The agency handled participant recruiting based on our screener, which freed us to focus on the experience of both our users and our colleagues. We invited everyone: product managers, engineers, marketers, customer support leads, and the executive leadership team. To make it more enticing, we set it up as an evening "watch party," complete with a casual dinner buffet. (Never underestimate the power of food to bring people together.)

For many, it was the first time they had seen someone outside the company use our products. They watched users struggle, hesitate, and sometimes give up. But they also witnessed moments of delight, clever workarounds, and appreciation for what we had done right.

People laughed, frowned, whispered reactions, and scribbled notes. My favorite moments came when test subjects asked, "Could you make it work like *this*?" When asked this question, my answer is always, "Is that the way you would like it to work?" This response always unleashed a cascade of stories from the customer's career: descriptions of job pressures, frustrations, accountabilities, and personal goals. Those insights gave us more context than any survey or analytics dashboard ever could.

These watch parties did more than test products. They built bridges across departments, created a shared understanding, and reframed UX as a collective responsibility. Most importantly, they reminded everyone that behind every product is a real person trying to accomplish something that matters to them.

The Lesson: Make Usability Testing an Event

Usability testing has greater impact when it becomes a shared experience rather than an isolated UX activity. Inviting colleagues across departments sparks serious discussions, fosters empathy, and helps establish UX as central to both customer satisfaction and business success.

Call to Action: Plan Your Next Usability Test

Partner with a market research firm. Search the web for market research facilities in your area. Check out their websites and call them to get details on the research spaces they offer. Provide a screener and let them handle recruiting, scheduling, and catering.

Schedule two days of sessions. I had success scheduling late afternoon to early evening sessions in 1-hour blocks: about 40 minutes for the test, and 20 minutes to debrief and set up for the next session.

Recruit five to six participants per day. This ensures coverage even if a few people cancel. Offer an honorarium of $100 or so.

Set up a sign-up sheet. Publicize the event and invite key team members and executives to observe. Have them sign up for one or both days.

Engage observers after each test. Go back to the observation room and ask if anyone has a question they would like you to ask.

Follow a script but stay flexible. Consistency is important, but let conversations flow. When participants ask, "Could it work like …?", turn the question back to them for richer insights.

Dealing with Customer Gatekeepers
Guardians at the Gate

At one company, we built highly specialized and expensive equipment. Customers needed formal training and hands-on

experience before they could use our products effectively. To support this, the company operated a dedicated demo and training center, a fully equipped space where customers could explore products with expert guidance.

The demo center seemed like the perfect place to conduct research. It required no travel budget and offered direct exposure to both products and customers. Training sessions provided opportunities to observe how new users interacted with the equipment and exposed features that were difficult to understand. And when no training was scheduled, the center allowed me to sit down and experience the equipment firsthand and "walk in the users' shoes."

One afternoon, during a quiet period with no sessions scheduled, I went to the center to analyze the product experience for myself. Within minutes, the demo center manager confronted me and insisted I leave. He was emphatic: employees were not allowed in unless they were running demos for customers!

I have seen this territoriality throughout my career: access to products and customers is often tightly controlled. Gatekeepers—demo staff, sales teams, support personnel, or even product managers—can view these touchpoints as their exclusive domain. Their instinct is to protect their turf rather than share it, even when collaboration with UX research would greatly benefit the company.

The Lesson: Build Access Through Respect

Access to products and customers is not automatic. Gaining it depends on cooperation with internal gatekeepers who control those relationships. The key is to show respect for their roles, explain your intentions, and demonstrate how your work supports their goals as much as your own. Without these allies, research will remain limited, and customer problems will stay hidden.

Call to Action: Partner with Gatekeepers

Identify the owners of key customer touchpoints. Map the roles inside your organization that interact most directly with customers, such as trainers, demo staff, support managers, sales reps, and account executives. These are the gatekeepers who can either block or enable UX research.

Engage early. Meet with these gatekeepers and explain your goals, describe what you will and will not do, and invite them to observe or participate. Early conversations create transparency and build credibility.

Clarify scheduling rules. Ask who should set up customer interactions. Some gatekeepers will prefer to schedule them; others may allow you to reach out directly. Either way, publish your plans and share research notes openly to reinforce collaboration. Respect their rules of engagement.

Reassure them about promises. Gatekeepers often worry that UX will make commitments to customers that can't be delivered. Make it clear you will never promise features or timelines. Your role is to listen, learn, and report.

Share credit. Recognize the contribution of gatekeepers when presenting findings. Show how their support made product improvements possible. This acknowledgment strengthens the relationship and makes future access easier.

Research Is Completed and Forgotten
The Treasure We Buried

Research was generously supported. Field visits were encouraged, usability testing was funded, sales presentations included UX, and attending conferences for vetting new concepts was a normal part of the calendar. As a researcher, it was an ideal environment.

We gathered an extraordinary volume of insights. We had handwritten notes, OneNote notebooks, Word documents, photos of customer setups, physical artifacts, and hours of recorded interviews. The result was a goldmine of raw data that could have shaped the future of the product in powerful ways.

Yet in ideation sessions, roadmap meetings, and Agile story definition summits, most of our research went unused because we lacked a central research repository to store our research notes and artifacts. There was no central database, no tagging system, and no process for making the insights searchable. Each researcher kept files in personal folders, and valuable findings were buried or forgotten. Busy teams had no time to sift through it all, and leaders did not invest in tools or infrastructure to make it accessible.

The result? Despite all the resources spent on research, the insights we gathered rarely influenced decisions. The effort generated knowledge, but without organization and follow-through, that knowledge never reached the people who needed it most.

The Lesson: Make Research Accessible and Actionable

Collecting research is only the first step. Without a way to organize, share, and apply insights, the effort is wasted. Research has impact only when it is easy to find, easy to use, and directly tied to decision-making. A repository—whether a commercial platform, a lightweight internal tool, or even a shared database—turns raw data into collective knowledge and makes it available when and where it is needed.

Call to Action: Operationalize Your Research

Create a centralized repository. Store notes, recordings, transcripts, and findings in one accessible system. Use commercially available platforms like Dovetail, Aurelius, or Condens, or work with development teams to build a lightweight in-house solution.

Leverage automation. Use transcription and AI tools to summarize notes, highlight patterns, and generate action items automatically. This reduces the burden of synthesis and accelerates the flow of insights to teams.

Conduct research in pairs. Have one person facilitate the session and the other capture notes. This approach improves accuracy and frees the facilitator to focus fully on the participant.

Record with permission. With participant consent, capture audio or video of research sessions. Transcriptions create searchable archives that preserve insights for future use.

Make insights visible. Share highlight reels, short summaries, and curated findings so stakeholders can quickly absorb key points without digging through raw data.

Prepare for key meetings. Extract insights and supporting data from your repository before ideation sessions, roadmap planning, and story definition. But also have the repository at the ready on your laptop to extract data and insights as conversations evolve.

Discovering Game-Changing Redesigns
"It's Just an Idea"

Whenever I start a new position with a company, my listening tour always includes customers. Internal stakeholders can provide

valuable context, but customers are the ones living with the product every day. They know what is and is not working.

In one role, I accompanied one of our implementation specialists to a customer site to conduct follow-up training. The customer had received training only a few weeks earlier, but had since forgotten everything when she finally got around to using the product. She came prepared with a notebook, determined to create a "cheat sheet" with step-by-step instructions for common tasks.

At the end of the session, she commented that the product was harder to use than it should be. She called it the "clicky system" because of all the mouse clicks required to get the result she wanted. Then she described, in plain terms, exactly how she wished it would work.

Instead of layers of menus and links, she wanted to see a representation of her business domain, including all the objects she worked with on a daily basis and all the actions she wanted to perform on those objects. When she finished describing her dream product, she ended with a humble remark: "It's just an idea."

That comment revealed a big unmet customer need and reframed my vision for the product. It was not a feature request; it was an insight that sparked a complete reimagining of our flagship product. The redesign that followed became one of the most rewarding efforts of my career. It transformed the customer experience and established new credibility for the UX team.

The Lesson: Customer Insights Are Innovation Catalysts

Customers live with problems and the workarounds every day. Their words often expose blind spots that teams overlook. They may not propose polished solutions, but their plain descriptions of what they need can inspire breakthroughs. Listening carefully without bias can surface opportunities that change the direction of a product and even the trajectory of a business.

Call to Action: Turning Observation into Impact

Attend training and consulting sessions. Contact the leaders of your training and consulting departments and explain that you'd like to tag along as part of your user research. Agree to ground rules about asking questions and getting feedback. Ask to be kept informed of upcoming engagements during on-site visits and attend as your budget and schedule allow.

Observe in-house training sessions. When customers come to your site, sit quietly at the back of the room and watch body language and engagement. Do they look puzzled? Do they repeatedly ask for help? These cues reveal learning barriers. Ask open-ended questions before they leave to surface deeper insights.

Record responsibly. Capture video or audio when possible, making sure to secure consent and avoid personally identifiable information. Recordings let you revisit details later and share unfiltered moments with colleagues who could not attend.

Prototype solutions to observed issues. Do not stop at identifying problems. Create quick-win prototypes for immediate improvements and strategic prototypes for long-term fixes. Acknowledge how collaboration with your training department has led to numerous insights and improvements in UX.

Prepare for transformative redesigns. Occasionally, one comment will point to something that requires more than incremental fixes. Be ready to lead bold redesign efforts when the evidence supports it. These are career-defining opportunities.

Customer Rebellions
A Front-Row Seat to Frustration

One of the most powerful ways to expose critical UX bugs is to watch people use your product in their own environment. No agenda. Just real people, doing real work. These moments reveal issues that would never surface in a formal interview or lab test.

Shortly after we launched a new product, I sat in on a hands-on, customer training session. A room full of new customers were introduced to the product for the first time, and I joined a support consultant who was there to resolve issues and answer questions. Within minutes, nearly every hand in the room was raised. Users were confused, stuck in the middle of their tasks, unable to proceed, and dependent on the consultant for help. He was quickly overwhelmed, moving from workstation to workstation, trying to keep up.

This was not an edge case. It was a widespread breakdown. The problem was not usability flaws in isolation, but also reliability and performance issues. If customers were this confused in a controlled training environment with help at hand, what would happen when they used the product on their own?

When we shared recordings of the session, it was clear to everyone that we had released this MVP before it was ready. It was a beta, not a product.

We paused shipments and scrambled to fix the problems. Had we not seen these issues for ourselves, we could have lost millions of dollars in product return costs and irreparably damaged the brand.

The Lesson: MVPs Can Be Dangerous

A Minimum Viable Product (MVP) may deliver on functional requirements, but if the user experience is weak, the consequences can be severe. Paying customers who face repeated frustration will lose trust, spread negative word-of-mouth, and in some cases, abandon the product for a competitor. Good usability at launch is essential to sustain credibility and customer loyalty.

Call to Action: Managing MVP Risk

Limit early exposure to new products. Release MVPs only to trusted customers who understand the risks. Provide on-site support during the early weeks and monitor feedback closely. Rapid fixes and quick iterations are essential to maintain trust.

Test before release, even under pressure. Conduct usability tests and a complete UX analysis prior to launch and allow sufficient time for fixing serious pain points. Document critical flaws and present a clear go/no-go recommendation to leadership. Even if overruled, you will be on record for warning your colleagues of the potential risks of going ahead with the release.

Prepare to act in crisis mode. If post-launch feedback turns negative, mobilize the UX team to lead recovery. Work side by side with development in rapid cycles to prioritize fixes, validate changes, and release updates quickly.

Respond to frustrated customers with empathy. Acknowledge customer frustration and demonstrate your commitment to addressing the issues they raise. Trust can be rebuilt when customers see pain points addressed quickly and transparently.

Celebrating Design Research Wins
When Research Reveals Customer Delight

Sometimes the most valuable insight from a customer visit isn't discovering what is broken, but seeing what is working

exceptionally well.

After adding gamification features to one of our products, we arranged a visit with a long-term customer. About twenty employees gathered in a conference room to try it out. We divided them into teams, explained the new features, and let them play.

The response was incredible. Teams collaborated on strategies, laughed, cheered when they won, and groaned when they lost. The energy in the room was joyful and authentic. It was the kind of engagement every designer hopes for but rarely witnesses so vividly.

We asked permission to record the session and later shared the videos across the company. Even skeptical stakeholders smiled as they watched. The product team was celebrated for delivering something impactful, and other teams were encouraged to follow the example.

But the impact extended beyond the office. Sales teams reported that the gamification features quickly became a major selling point, helping us win deals against competitors. The financial results confirmed what the customer visit had shown: this was a feature that customers loved and the market noticed.

The Lesson: Balancing Critique with Praise

Critiquing flaws is a central responsibility of our profession, but it is just as important to recognize and celebrate successes. Highlighting what works strengthens partnerships and shifts the perception of design research from a function that only points out problems to one that celebrates successes. A balanced approach to sharing both pain points and delighters encourages cross-functional collaboration and removes your colleagues' dread of hearing only negative research findings.

Call to Action: Share the Credit for UX Wins

Highlight success, not just problems. Create videos that showcase what is working, not only what needs fixing. Showing customer excitement demonstrates the value of good UX in enhancing customer loyalty.

Turn positive feedback into a shared experience. When you know a design works well, schedule observation sessions that capture customer delight. Invite the entire team, including executives, to watch firsthand.

Share the spotlight. Recognize that good outcomes result from collaboration. Credit the entire product team: developers, product managers, and designers. Visible recognition is the best way to recruit allies to the UX cause.

Broadcast wins across the company. Share recordings at all-hands meetings, on your intranet, in your team newsletter, and during release celebrations.

Work with marketing to publicize great UX achievements. Marketing is always looking for good stories to put on the company website and include in their marcom literature. Make sure they are aware of the wins your research has revealed.

Co-Sponsoring Customer Events
Set Up a Board of Advisors

One of the most effective ways I have found to stay connected to users is by partnering with product management to create a

customer advisory board. When done well, it becomes a powerful bridge between the people building the product and the people using it.

Once a year, we flew in a handpicked group of key customers for a two-day, in-person advisory board event at our headquarters. Company employees gave a few short presentations, but the spotlight was on the customers. They shared how they were using our products with the other attendees, often in ways we had not anticipated. They described the workarounds they had invented, the obstacles they had faced, and the successes they had achieved. It was energizing, enlightening, and sometimes humbling.

These structured sessions delivered useful insights, but the most valuable moments came between presentations. Casual conversations during breaks and chats over lunch afforded people opportunities to share candid perspectives with us that rarely surface in a formal setting.

Not every company can afford to fly customers to in-person sessions. A virtual advisory board that meets quarterly or monthly can also be effective. We used them to strengthen relationships, test early ideas, and gather ideas for new features.

The Lesson: Co-Design with Your Best Customers

Turning a customer base into a connected community strengthens relationships and drives product direction. Board members value opportunities to share with one another, learn best practices, and highlight their successes. Facilitating these exchanges, whether in-person or virtually, gives your company a chance to showcase recent design initiatives, solicit direct feedback, and gather fresh ideas from engaged users. More than any marketing message, they demonstrate a real commitment to the statement: "Designed by customers, for customers."

Call to Action: Build a Customer Community

Propose a customer outreach program. If none exists, product management and UX should work together to create one. Sell the idea as a collaborative effort that deepens relationships, builds loyalty, and yields richer feedback.

Identify high-value participants. Partner with sales and customer success teams to select participants. Prioritize long-term customers, strategic accounts, and those who have found innovative ways to deploy your products.

Start small with virtual events. Launch with monthly online sessions. Keep them short, engaging, and focused on real customer stories and early product ideas.

Scale up to annual in-person gatherings. As the program demonstrates value, invest in annual events at company headquarters or local venues. Cover travel costs for invited customers and encourage them to present their own use cases. Rotate participants annually to keep perspectives fresh.

Research Reporting with Influence and Impact
From Reports to Reels: Making Research Matter

When I began conducting user research in the 1990s, the gold standard was the formal report. Every research program ended

with a long document that included an executive summary, background, methodology, task scenarios, findings, recommendations, and next steps. These reports took weeks to prepare. They looked impressive, but almost no one read them. At best, they checked the box that research had been done. At worst, they had no influence at all.

The purpose of user research is not to generate paperwork. Its purpose is to uncover insights, reveal problems, and propose solutions that inspire action. Over time, we realized that our traditional reports were failing to achieve this purpose.

We shifted to shorter, more engaging formats. Instead of long documents, we created one-page infographics that distilled the essence of our findings. We printed them as posters and encouraged employees to hang them in their cubicles. This allowed us to literally point to the issues when discussing design changes. The visuals made the message stick.

We also used video. An in-product support manager on our team was skilled in video editing and created short highlights reels from usability tests. Each reel ran only three to five minutes and captured the most compelling moments of success and frustration. We shared them at all-hands meetings, posted them internally, and used them at team offsites. Usability issues were no longer abstractions—they were real, visible, and impossible to ignore.

The Lesson: Apply UX Design to Research Reporting

The influence of research is not derived from the formality of its methodology or the length of its report. It comes from how well insights inspire action. Long documents may look impressive, but they're boring.

Visual summaries and highlight reels, on the other hand, capture attention and drive conversation. Findings must be packaged in ways that are engaging, easy to share, and incite discussions among team members and executives about ways to solve problems that have been revealed.

Call to Action: Reimagine Research Communications

Replace long reports with concise visuals. Use single-page summaries or infographics to highlight key insights. Post them in your team space and encourage others to post them as well. If you have a physical kanban or scrum board, post the infographic next to it as a constant reminder of pain points that need to be solved.

Show, don't just tell. Create short highlight reels of research activities (usability tests, customer interviews, observational research). Make them available online on your team webpage in the corporate intranet.

Tell stories. Don't just present research data—frame findings as narratives with problems and calls to action. Create quick prototypes of potential solutions that dramatize the difference between the current experience and the potential future experience.

When Research Data Lies
Observe and Analyze

Scott Cook, when Chairman of the Executive Committee at Intuit, once shared a story that illustrates how easily research data can

mislead us. Intuit had run usability tests on TurboTax, confident that the results would validate its ease of use. And they did. The numbers looked great: tasks were completed, error rates were low, and users reported satisfaction. By every traditional metric, the product appeared successful.

Then Intuit took the next step. They conducted in-home studies and watched real people prepare their actual tax returns. That's when the cracks appeared. Away from the lab, outside of the artificial structure of assigned tasks, users stumbled. They grew confused and made mistakes that the usability test didn't reveal. The usability test data had painted a picture of success, but the reality was far more nuanced.

Many so-called "representative users" recruited for lab tests have spent years accommodating bad design. In a controlled environment, they perform well—not because the product is well designed, but because they have adapted to its complexity. The quantitative report looks good, but it fails to tell the whole story.

To avoid this trap, I developed a technique I called an Information Inventory. I broke down a task into every action the user needed to complete and listed every piece of information they would need to find in order to successfully perform each action. Then I evaluated each required action and piece of information using three metrics: relevance, findability, and effectiveness. This analysis exposed weak points in the experience that would likely lead to failure in a usability test.

The Lesson: Trust Your Instincts

Usability data can create a false sense of confidence in your design. Metrics may suggest success, but numbers alone can't assess the full experience in a real-world setting. Users who perform well in lab tests often do so because they have adapted to design flaws, not because the design is easy to use. If we stop our research at the lab, we risk mistaking endurance for satisfaction. The market will eventually correct us, but by then it's too late.

Great design requires going beyond metrics. It requires stepping into the customer's world, observing them in real conditions, and noticing what the data hides: hesitation, body language, and learned workarounds. UX research involves subjective observation, not just numerical validation.

Call to Action: Look Beyond the Data

Observe real users using your products in real settings. Don't conduct usability tests with representative users and think your research is complete. Find a way to conduct observational field studies, ideally at your customer's site, or virtually through a video conferencing app.

Perform an in-depth user experience analysis for critical tasks. UX analysis is one of the most underutilized activities in user research. List all steps users are required to perform to achieve a common task, and every bit of information they must either know or find before they can perform each action.

Then ask three questions:

1. From the user's perspective, is this action relevant to the result they are trying to achieve, or does it feel like an unnecessary diversion?
2. Does a typical user already know this information, or will they have to suspend their quest for a result to search for it?
3. Once found, is this information easy to understand and allow the user to complete the action?

Chapter 2: Inspiring Your Colleagues

UX has never been a solitary craft, though many of us entered it because we loved the quiet work of problem-solving and design. We live in the world of ideas, where a long stretch of uninterrupted time to pursue a cascade of solutions can feel like bliss. But in every company I've worked for, I've learned that even the most elegant design can fail if you don't have allies.

Early in my career, I would disappear into my own head, sketching, prototyping, and refining until I had what I thought was the perfect solution. Then I'd unveil it, only to discover that my colleagues in development, marketing, or product management were openly hostile to me and my solution. They hadn't been part of the journey, and without their support, even great designs would die in a meeting room.

It took me years to understand that success in UX isn't just about insight or craft; it's about influence and inspiration. It's about helping others open their eyes to see a problem that only you can see and, more importantly, helping them see *their own role* in solving it. When people feel their fingerprints are on the final product, they become its champions.

In this chapter, I share stories of both success and failure—times when collaboration turned skeptics into believers, and other times when I was defeated by the corporate immune system. More than teamwork and influence, *inspiration* is required to activate an entire organization in the quest to achieve a world-class user experience.

Convincing Defenders of the Current Design
Coming "Late to the Party"

In several roles throughout my career, I was brought in as the very first UX professional the company had ever hired. Most of these

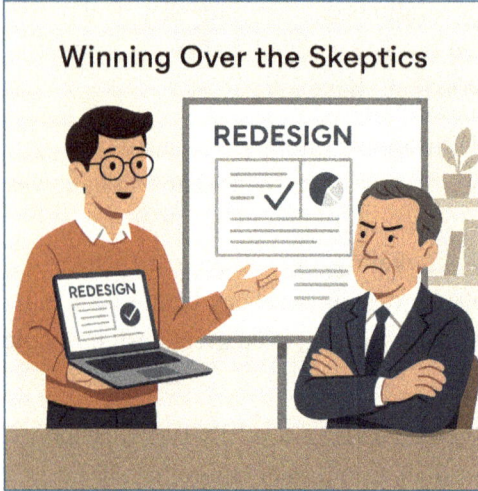

organizations did not fully understand what UX was; they simply knew they needed it.

In one case, a leader admitted that my hiring was just to "speak UX" in meetings with partner organizations that already had mature design practices. My challenge was proving the value of UX in a setting where no one had seen it in action before.

I began with a UX audit of the flagship product. In low-maturity organizations, this is often where tension begins. Questioning long-standing design decisions can quickly create defensiveness. At this company, after I suggested that the flagship product could benefit from an extensive redesign, an executive dismissed the idea with a sharp "Oh, sure. You're late to the party and don't understand why we designed it that way."

Too late I remembered a lesson I had learned long ago that showing is more persuasive than telling, so to recover from this disappointing first meeting, I created a simple mockup that demonstrated how the product could be faster, simpler, and easier to use. It worked. The same executive who originally dismissed my suggestion became one of the redesign's strongest champions.

By visually comparing the current state to the proposed future state, my colleagues saw the value UX could bring to the party, even if we were late.

The Lesson: Build Trust Before You Critique

In immature UX cultures, honest critiques won't win over your partners. Do the research, build prototypes, and walk stakeholders through how your proposed designs simplify the experience and highlight the product's strengths. Then support those prototypes with a thorough design audit that details how the current design can be enhanced to better serve your customers' needs. When people can see and experience the benefits of a product refresh firsthand, they are more likely to support it.

Call to Action: Seek First to Understand Past Decisions

Ask for the story behind the product. Seeking first to understand the technical constraints, schedule pressures, and resource limitations that produced the current product lets your colleagues know that you appreciate and empathize with the pressures they were under.

Lead with positivity. Start every UX audit presentation by pointing out what works well. Recognize effective features and acknowledge the effort behind them. This goodwill reduces defensiveness and establishes a safe space for honest critique.

Frame opportunities in context. In engineering-driven cultures, praise technical excellence before suggesting UX refinements. Position your recommendations as ways to maximize adoption and return on that technical investment.

Start small for quick wins. Even if you uncover many issues, focus first on a few high-impact, easy-to-fix improvements. Early wins build credibility and open the door for larger initiatives.

Use evidence to tackle systemic issues. Once trust is established, introduce more complex challenges. Support your recommendations with customer quotes, journey maps, prototypes, or usability data to make the problems and solutions tangible.

Allaying Fears of Over Promising
Vetting New Concepts Without Promising Them

In many organizations, product managers, sales teams, and developers hesitate to share early design concepts with customers.

Showing preliminary ideas can create the impression that a feature is promised, leading to unrealistic customer expectations and disappointment when it does not make it into the next release.

Despite the risk, early feedback on new concepts has proven essential in my research efforts, but setting expectations—both with customers and with stakeholders—is critical. When I shared early ideas, I made it clear that these were concepts under exploration, not committed features, and that some may never progress beyond this stage. I framed the discussion as a collaborative exercise: "We are trying to understand which ideas could potentially make your work easier."

Transparency made this research possible. Customers no longer worried about timelines. Instead, they engaged with the ideas, shared candid reactions, and contributed constructively to shaping the product's future direction. Stakeholders relaxed, assured that the proper context was established before asking for feedback.

In continuous discovery, the debate over whether to use wireframes or polished prototypes should be driven by research goals, not philosophical principles. Low-fidelity sketches help teams focus on interaction flows and information hierarchy. High-fidelity models reveal the emotional and aesthetic impact. With today's tools, either option can be produced quickly.

I personally have had more success with production-quality interactive simulations. I've found the feedback to be much richer when customers see how the new features seamlessly fit within the current product's design framework. By including "dummy data" in the prototypes instead of generic boxes and "Lorem Ipsum" text, customers can better imagine what the experience of using the new feature would be like in their day-to-day work.

The Lesson: Test Early Concepts, But Set Expectations

Sharing concepts early requires care, but the benefits outweigh the risks. Begin each customer feedback session with a caveat that what they are about to see is only an idea for the purpose of gauging its usefulness to customers. Emphasize that prototypes are experiments, only a small fraction of which make it to market. And if a prototype does survive to deployment, it will likely look and behave very differently from what they are about to see.

Call to Action: Get Early Concept Feedback Carefully

Collaborate on a unified customer script. Before meeting with customers, partner with product management, development, and sales to develop a script that frames early concepts as exploratory. Use clear language to set expectations: there is no release date and no guarantee of delivery. The purpose is to understand potential usefulness and adoption.

Invite cross-functional stakeholders. Include product managers, account representatives, and developers in customer sessions. Hearing reactions firsthand reassures them that you are following the agreed-upon script when presenting new concepts and helps them judge what the impact on sales might be if the new feature is implemented.

Record and share feedback. Capture reactions through notes, quotes, and recordings. Summarize findings so the broader team can see evidence that led to design decisions. Capturing feedback strengthens the case for continuing to refine promising ideas and to abandon weak ones.

When Starting Over Is the Right Call
Profiles in Courage

Early in my career, my company partnered with another firm to co-develop a web portal. Our partner had fully embraced human-

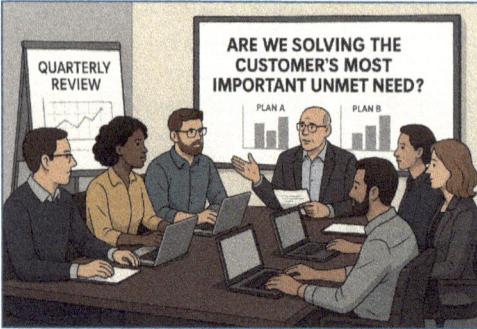

centered design as a discipline that guided every decision. By contrast, my company was still operating with an engineering-first mindset. Working across corporate cultures was like stepping into a parallel universe where customer insight set the direction instead of technical requirements.

One of their practices was especially courageous. Every quarter, they brought together product teams and senior leaders for status updates and to ask a single question: *Are we truly solving the customer's big unmet need?* If the answer was no, they did not hesitate to adjust their approach regardless of the impact to the schedule. Even with deadlines approaching, they were willing to pivot until they could be confident they were delivering genuine value.

I once witnessed that same courage at another company. A product was scheduled to launch in time for the busy holiday sales season. As was his practice, the CEO test drove it himself before release. Within minutes, he discovered that the installation process was too complex for the average customer. He delayed the launch by three months to fix this major usability flaw.

Why did he do this? Because he knew that shortly after the holidays customers would be lining up at stores to return the unusable product. The projected costs of returns outweighed the upside of holiday sales. The decision also prevented brand damage and long-term losses in market share.

In today's Agile environments, "go/no-go" reviews may seem outdated, but they can prevent a lot of negative consequences down the road. After every sprint, teams should pause to ask: *Does this feature meet the customer's need?* It's a simple question, but it keeps organizations grounded and helps prevent warranty and support disasters after launch.

The Lesson: The Courage to Reassess

Admitting that a current experience does not address the customer's critical need requires exceptional courage. Sometimes small adjustments are insufficient. Success may demand starting over, conducting more research, performing deeper analysis, and exploring new concepts. Although this can consume time and resources, the cost of pressing ahead with a flawed approach is often much greater, both in customer loyalty and business impact.

UX professionals can provide an essential service by surfacing critical flaws with evidence and data. Still, gaining acceptance for major changes and schedule impacts depends on a culture that values decision making based on both human-centered *and* business criteria.

Call to Action: Validate the Experience Before Release

Perform a thorough pre-release UX analysis. Evaluate major tasks and measure the time, effort, and ease required for customers to achieve results. Present these findings to stakeholders to help them decide whether the product is ready for release.

Quantify the business impact of poor UX. Work with customer support to estimate the financial consequences of usability issues, including projected returns, and call volumes. Translate user problems into dollar costs to make the case more persuasive.

Benchmark against competitors. Compare your product to its closest rivals on critical customer journeys. Focus on outcomes rather than features. If your product does not have parity or clearly lead in usability and simplicity, you have evidence of an unmet need that must be addressed before launch.

Listening Before Leading
Taking the Pulse of the Organization

Whenever I step into a new role, my first priority is not to suggest changes but to listen. I conduct a listening tour with executives

and influential individual contributors to understand current attitudes toward UX.

I begin by asking my manager for a list of people who shape the prevailing attitudes about UX and where it stands in the company's priorities. I then schedule thirty-minute conversations with each, keeping the tone casual and exploratory.

I introduce myself, explain my role, and ask questions like:

- What does your job look like day to day?
- What does success mean for you and your team?
- What challenges keep you up at night?
- When it comes to UX, what are your hopes, expectations, or concerns?

I take careful notes but I don't react to what I'm hearing. Instead, I go back to my desk, analyze patterns, look for opportunities where UX can address concerns, and distill one or two specific ideas for collaboration. I always close the loop by returning with a summary of what I heard and a proposal for how we might work together.

Taking the pulse of the organization signals that UX is not an isolated discipline but a partner in solving shared problems. And every strong partnership begins with listening.

The Lesson: Understand What Drives Your Partners

Influence begins with communicating that UX exists to help both customers *and* company leaders succeed. By listening before acting, you discover how the organization really works, where power lies, and what your colleagues value. Sharing back what you heard and proposing small, targeted actions demonstrates your desire to collaborate. This approach positions UX as a partner rather than a critic.

Call to Action: Profile Your Colleagues Like Customers

Begin with a strategic contact list. Request names of key influencers and respected contributors from your manager. Be sure to include both formal roles and informal networks.

Schedule thirty-minute conversations. Send email invitations describing who you are and explaining that you want to learn about their role, their goals, and their perspectives. Include sample questions in the invite to help them understand the topics you want to discuss.

During the meeting, keep the focus on them. Don't evangelize the value of UX, but encourage them to talk about their personal passions and concerns. Give a brief history of your experience to establish your credibility, but stay humble. Ask them to tell stories and provide examples of recent challenges they've faced and successes they've had. Ask the sample questions you provided in your invite, but let the conversation flow organically.

Express gratitude and keep the door open. Thank each participant sincerely, explain that you will be spending the next few weeks synthesizing input across all the conversations you're having, and ask for permission to follow up. Also ask if there is anyone else in their department that you should talk to.

Close the loop with outcomes. Reconnect later with a summary of what you learned, how their input informed your perspective, and one tangible idea that you would like to collaborate on.

User Empathy by Developers Desired, Not Required
Relate to Developers on Their Own Terms

We often say that UX is everybody's responsibility. But not everyone believes it, and some actively resist the idea.

At one company, my team organized a half-day workshop to introduce colleagues to core UX principles, services, and methods. We invited product managers, call center agents, and developers. The session was hands-on, with Gamestorming exercises, group discussions, and activities designed to make the concepts relevant across roles.

Most of the room was fully engaged. People shared ideas, asked thoughtful questions, and seemed to be enjoying themselves. But one developer sat in the back row with arms crossed and a frown fixed on his face. He refused to participate in any of the activities.

During a break, I asked him whether the session felt relevant to his work. He answered immediately: "I just want to go back to my desk and write code."

Clearly, our message had not reached him. He was not ready to accept his role in creating usable products that our customers wanted.

After this workshop, when engaging with developers, I learned to frame UX in engineering terms, presenting the user as a "human component" in the system architecture that must be designed with the same rigor as any other component. I argued that elegantly-coded features were a wasted effort if customers refused to use them because of their complexity.

The human component needed to be bug-free, just like the other components in the system, meaning that functionality assigned to humans must compile and execute without errors. This approach helped developers accept responsibility for coding usability into their deliverables.

The Lesson: Meet Your Colleagues Where They Are

Empathy is often encouraged in UX, but it is not strictly required to produce human-centered designs. Great design can also begin with systems thinking.

In engineering-driven organizations, one of the most effective ways to connect with developers is to frame the user as a vital component in the product system. Just as a software bug can crash an application, so can a failure in the human component. If people can't understand or operate the product, the brilliance of the code will never be appreciated.

Call to Action: Design the User Component

Include the human component in the system architecture. Treat the user as a component in the system and emphasize that any component, if designed incorrectly and assigned functions that it cannot perform, can cause the system to crash.

Express empathy for developers. If developers resist including UX design enhancements, appeal to their expertise and willingness to stand up to a challenge. Stress that you don't want their excellent work to go unnoticed or underutilized by users simply because the feature is too hard to use. Cite examples where features were ignored by customers if you can.

Celebrate developers who build innovative UX features. Publicize and reward their efforts. Show videos and collect testimonials showcasing customer delight with their work.

When Designs Are Challenged
Reviewers Feel Obligated to Find Something Wrong

In nearly every role I've held, there was an instance when someone challenged our design with an alternative they believed was better.

Sometimes the challenge is valid. A developer once shared an alternative concept with one of our junior UX designers. She knew his design was better, and I could see the unspoken question on her face: *If developers can improve on my design, what is my value here?*

I encouraged her to incorporate his design into the next iteration. I told her she would earn more credibility by acknowledging his contribution than by defending her professional territory. Recognizing his input strengthened her working relationship with the development team and demonstrated that UX was a collaborative, outcome-driven partner. Most importantly, it aligned with our responsibility to deliver the best possible user experience, regardless of whose idea it is.

But not every suggestion is an improvement. When invited to review a design, some people feel obligated to propose a change— any change. In those cases, we relied on data. We prototyped both versions and compared them using clear metrics: fewer clicks, clearer language, faster completion of tasks. These benchmarks were hard to argue with.

When metrics could not provide a decisive answer, we turned to users themselves. By testing alternatives in research sessions, we let customers guide the final decision. The result was a better product and a shared confidence in the process that produced it.

The Lesson: Let the Best Idea Win

Don't take design challenges personally. Keep an open mind and stay focused on delivering the best possible experience. Sometimes feedback leads to genuine improvement, sometimes it's neutral, and occasionally it makes the experience worse. Evaluate every suggestion objectively, using evidence and research to determine the right path.

In UX, the best idea can come from anywhere. Our responsibility is not to protect ownership of the design but to protect the quality of the experience.

Call to Action: Treat Design Challenges as Opportunities

Don't respond defensively. When colleagues suggest changes to your design concepts, acknowledge their input and let them know you will revisit the design after conducting a thorough comparative analysis.

Acknowledge good ideas. Recognize contributions from colleagues when their suggestions improve the experience. It is an excellent opportunity to win allies for future UX initiatives.

Differentiate useful feedback from noise. Use simple UX metrics to evaluate whether suggestions improve the design or just make it different but not better. Reviewers often provide feedback because they feel it's their job to do so, but they really don't care whether you follow it or not.

All things being equal, give a little. If the original design and the alternative design are equivalent in terms of usability, consider accepting the proposed change. You may win points for flexibility and gain allies in the process.

Let users decide. When evidence is inconclusive, test both approaches with real customers. Observation beats opinion.

Teaching Workshops
Teaching UX Principles Where They're Needed Most

In several global companies, I became known not only for practicing UX but also for teaching it. Many of these organizations

had very few UX professionals, sometimes none at all. Design decisions were largely made by engineers. They were smart, committed people who cared about making quality products, but they often lacked the tools to approach design from a human-centered perspective.

To address this, I began offering workshops tailored to developers and product managers. I studied the best ideas from current thought leaders and adapted them to the realities of fast-moving, engineering-driven environments. I also had the time and space to invent my own principles and methodologies. My goal was not to teach theory, but to provide pragmatic, hands-on approaches to human-centered design that fit within tight schedules and resource constraints.

The result was a two-day interactive workshop that guided teams through a process of identifying and solving design challenges with lightweight, actionable methods. I did not expect engineers to become designers. Instead, I wanted them to walk away with tools and mindsets that would help them make their own work more human-centered without slowing down development.

The Lesson: Reframe UX for Your Audience

To influence culture, you must frame UX in terms that resonate outside the design world. The most effective teaching introduces new ways of thinking, new models, and new frameworks that solve real problems—both for colleagues and for customers.

Workshops must also be short, relevant, and immediately applicable. Few teams can afford to abandon their jobs for a week of theory. Training activities must be entertaining as well as impactful, and lead to insights that end up on product roadmaps and Agile backlogs. Your goal is not just to educate your teammates, but to *inspire* them to contribute innovative solutions to big customer needs.

Call to Action: Become a UX Thought Leader

Learn from the best. Watch how great facilitators structure their workshops, keep energy high, and draw people into the process. Notice slide design, storytelling, humor, and authenticity. Borrow what works and make it your own.

Use real examples. Ground your sessions in your company's products and challenges so participants see the immediate relevance of UX principles.

Create space for discovery. Do not lecture. Ask questions, pause, and let participants wrestle with the answers. That's how "*Aha!*" breakthroughs happen.

Expand UX's reach. Invite product managers, engineers, and others outside the design team. The more people recognize their part in delivering great UX, the stronger your organization becomes.

Make it fun, especially for yourself. You need to enjoy what you teach. I use video clips from movies, clever anecdotes, inspirational stories, and a UX Hall of Shame to entertain both my audience and myself. I love seeing the audience's reaction when a presentation works.

Contrasting the Before and After
Exposing the Past, Envisioning the Future

It's one thing to argue that a new design is better. It is another thing entirely to *prove* it by letting people experience the "before"

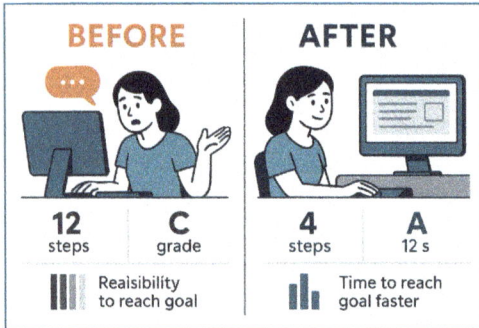

and "after" side by side, with clear metrics that make your case undeniable. The old UX mantra "show, don't tell" still holds true.

I applied this principle when proposing a breakthrough redesign of a legacy product. We had conducted user research that uncovered painful challenges, and I knew our metrics and findings alone would not be compelling. So, I staged a dramatic story to present to the Executive Leadership Team.

I began with a short video clip of a customer describing how frustrating the current experience was in her own words. Then I walked the leadership team through three critical tasks, highlighting the complex navigation, unnecessary steps, and confusion that defined the current flow. Rather than just describing problems, I invited my colleagues to experience them.

Next I showed a prototype of the proposed future state. I stressed that it was preliminary and co-created with product management and development, but I used the same three tasks to demonstrate how the new design worked. Task by task, they saw how much simpler, faster, and more intuitive the journey had become.

But vision alone does not fund a project. I explained how support calls related to those tasks were costing the company significant money. I presented a competitive analysis showing that our rivals were already ahead in usability, making us vulnerable in the market. And I reframed the redesign as not just a nice thing to do but a business imperative.

The turning point came when I reassured leadership that the new experience would not cannibalize existing sales of legacy products. It would expand them. That final piece tipped the balance. What began as a proposal ended with a green light to proceed.

The Lesson: Tell a Story, Then Rewrite How the Story Ends

Leaders and stakeholders are bombarded with data, decks, and opinions every day, but these rarely change minds. What cuts through is a vivid contrast: the pain of the current state set against the clarity of the future state. When people see the inefficiency, confusion, and frustration of the old design, and then experience the simplicity and delightfulness of the new one, you have their attention. Close by tying UX outcomes directly to business outcomes—including support call volume, competitive benchmarks, and sales opportunities—and the case is irrefutable.

Call to Action: Help Your Audience Feel Pain, Then Joy

Stage the story, don't just tell it. Use video clips, highlight reels, and live walkthroughs to make your audience feel the pain of the current experience. Contrast it directly with a prototype of your future vision. The difference will speak louder than bullets and charts on a PowerPoint slide.

Anchor the future design to business impact. Translate usability improvements into metrics executives value, such as reduced support costs, increased sales, lower churn, or competitive advantage. Make the ROI visible.

Anticipate leadership concerns. Address objections like budget, cannibalization of current products, and timelines before they surface. Removing doubt is as important as building excitement.

Close with a clear ask. End with a direct request for funding, resources, or sponsorship. Make it easy for leaders to commit.

Using the Competition for Dramatic Leverage
Turning Competitive Analysis into a Wake-Up Call

There are many ways to conduct a UX competitive analysis. In one project, I built a simple comparison table: five columns for our

key competitors and ten rows for the attributes I wanted to measure. Access to competitor products was limited, so I pieced together what I could by studying websites, reviewing screenshots and marketing materials, analyzing documentation, and watching YouTube videos posted by real users. It was not perfect, but it provided enough detail to sketch out how each product handled core tasks.

To make the results easy to read, I scored each attribute with visual markers: a filled circle for strong UX, a half-filled circle for partial coverage, and an empty circle for weak experiences. I added our own product to the table so leaders could see how we compared. The table was clear and understandable, but it lacked emotional impact.

I decided to try a different approach. Instead of just presenting data, I built a prototype that addressed one of the most painful customer challenges. It looked like a finished product, but I branded it with our *competitor's* logo.

When I presented it, the reaction was abject fear. Leaders assumed our competitor had already moved ahead with a breakthrough design. Then I clicked a button. Slowly the competitor's logo faded away and was replaced with our own. Expressions of relief replaced their panic. I told them, "This does not have to be their story. It can be ours. But we have to act now!" Numbers are useful, but stories change minds.

The reveal was just as important as the story. Replacing a competitor's logo with our own turned anxiety into empowerment. It showed that the better experience was within our reach if we acted decisively. Blending data, design, and emotion created the momentum needed to look beyond the status quo toward a brighter future.

The Lesson: Sometimes You Have to Scare Them

Competitive analysis is more than comparing features. It is a form of storytelling. Data highlights strengths and weaknesses, but emotion motivates action. Fear of being left behind, urgency to seize opportunities, and the clarity of seeing what's possible drive decisions more effectively than charts alone.

Call to Action: Instill a Sense of Urgency

Conduct UX research on your competitors. Even if you can't test drive your competitors' products, you can mine a trove of information on their websites. You can find documentation on their support sites. YouTube often has video walkthroughs of products posted by customers.

Perform a UX competitive analysis on similar features. Analyze how many steps are required to complete key tasks, compare the visual design to your own, evaluate ease of navigation and findability, and give the product an overall UX score.

Turn competitive data into stories. Present findings as a narrative that leaders can connect to, not just charts and symbols.

Deliver emotion alongside reason. If your product is falling behind on UX metrics, find a way to scare your leadership into action. Show the gap in UX parity between your product and theirs. But don't leave leaders feeling helpless. Show how the problem can be solved and why your organization is perfectly positioned to take the lead in the marketplace.

Shifting the Organization's UX Mindset
Stop Calling Them "Users"

As advocates for human-centered design, one of our biggest responsibilities is challenging how our organizations think about the "U" in UX.

In one role as Director of User Experience Design, I lobbied to remove the word *user* from our vocabulary. Our team stopped calling ourselves the user experience team and became the experience design team. Some colleagues thought I was overreacting to a harmless word. But words shape how we think, and this one was holding us back.

To explain the reasoning behind the name change, I told a simple story. Imagine you are writing a report in Microsoft Word. At that moment, you identify as a *writer,* focused on ideas and how best to communicate them. Then, in the middle of your writing, you notice the page number is wrong, and you need to reset it back to page 1. You know the result you want, but you can't find the correct sequence of clicks among Word's many ribbons, menus, and toolbars.

In that instant, you stop being a writer. Word forces you to abandon your goal and become a *user*, someone forced to focus on technology instead of pursuing the task that matters.

We don't want to be users. We want to be writers. And our customers don't want to be users either.

In every meeting when the word user came up, I reminded my colleagues that we weren't designing for "users"—we were designing for people who have jobs, goals, and identities that matter more than their interaction with our products. Human-centered design means building experiences that let people stay in their chosen role, focused on the results that matter to them.

Every day, I worked to reinforce this mindset: we are not serving generic users. We are serving people. The sooner we drop the "U," the closer we come to building products for real people instead of generic abstractions.

The Lesson: There Are No Users

The words we use to describe the people we serve influence how organizations think about them. Calling someone a *user* reduces them to a willing actor who will learn what we tell them to learn, stripped of their identity and intent. Replacing that word with accountant, student, patient, writer, etc., reminds us that our work is about enabling human goals, not mastering technology.

Reframing language can be a powerful lever for culture change. Dropping the "U" in UX was not about semantics. It was a visible signal that our mission was bigger than interfaces. It reminded us that our goal was not to increase the number of minutes customers spent using our products, but was instead about helping real people focus on getting the results we promised them instead of distracting them with complex experiences.

Call to Action: Replace "Users" with Real People

Create named personas. Develop personas with names, photos, and quotes. Refer to them by name in meetings—e.g., "*Carlos* wants to submit an expense report"—instead of "the *user* wants to submit an expense report.".

Challenge your language. Replace "user" with terms that reflect real roles such as writer, student, or patient.

Tell grounding stories. Use examples from your research that show how your product's complexity interrupts people's goals and forces them into the role of "user."

Dispelling the Myth of the Super User
No One Wants to Master Your Product

A product owner came to me with what he believed was a breakthrough idea. His product was notoriously complex, packed

with features that surveys showed were rarely used. His solution was to create a "super user" certification course: over a dozen lessons that would transform customers into experts who had mastered even the most obscure features of the product.

I had been trying to convince the organization that customers did not want to be "users," let alone "super users." They were busy professionals who just wanted to launch our product, accomplish their tasks, and move on to their real jobs. The less time they spent inside our product, the better.

Still, he pushed forward, and I agreed to review his progress. After months of work, he produced a polished master class. He was convinced it would boost adoption, sales, and loyalty.

Three months after launch, he pulled the usage stats. Almost no one had completed the course. Only a small fraction of customers had even started it. His months of effort had little impact on customer behavior.

I empathized with him, but it gave me the chance to make a larger point: instead of asking customers to take time out of their busy days to become experts, we could embed small, contextual moments of guidance directly into the product, ensuring that information is delivered at the right time, in the right place, and in the medium they preferred to consume it. This became the seed of our omnichannel support strategy.

The Lesson: Your Product Is the Means, Not the Ends

Customers don't want to master your product. They want to master their jobs. The myth of the super user persists, but these beings rarely exist in reality. Customers don't want to earn badges or memorize every feature. They want to accomplish their work quickly and efficiently. Asking them to invest time in training shifts the burden onto them when the responsibility belongs to us as designers to reduce the need for training. If a product requires extensive lessons to unlock its value, the problem is the product's complexity, not the user's lack of knowledge.

Call to Action: Learning Is Not the Customer's Job

Transform your company's approach to training. Unless your users' job is to master your product and spend all day using it (e.g., a CT/MRI technician), propose embedding learning into your product designs. Build a strong relationship with your training and support teams and collaborate on integrating training directly into the product experience.

Employ new learning delivery methods. Replace long courses with contextual guidance like tooltips, guided walkthroughs, and short videos that appear at the moment of need.

Measure what matters. Track task success rates, time-to-completion, and reductions in support calls, not course enrollments or completions.

Create an executive-level UX position. Merge embedded support, content development, customer training, and experience design into one department under a Chief Experience Officer or VP of Experience. Wishful thinking, I know, but wouldn't that be wonderful?

Educate internally. Share stories like the failed super user course to remind stakeholders that customers are not aspiring experts. They are people with limited time who want to get their work done.

"If We're No Worse Than the Competition, We're OK"
The Problem of "Good Enough" UX

Early in my career, I heard an urban myth that stuck with me, supposedly attributed to a product manager: "As long as we

acquire customers faster than we can make them hate us, we're in business."

It sounded cynical and made up, but I learned later just how close to the truth it could be.

I once gave a presentation to a product manager, eager to make the case for UX. I was armed with statistics showing how companies that invested in UX earned a high ROI, how support costs dropped when experiences were simplified, and how usability could be a differentiator in our competitive marketplace. I thought I had built an airtight argument.

He listened politely. Then, at the end, he shrugged and said: "As long as we're no worse than our competitors, we really have no incentive to invest in UX."

I was stunned. At that point in my career, I was more of a zealot than a strategist and had assumed the benefits of UX were self-evident to everyone. I had not yet learned the most important lesson of UX evangelism: data alone does not persuade.

Over time, I got smarter. Instead of trying to argue abstract points, I built prototypes that *showed* the difference UX could make. I brought product managers along on user research visits so they could directly observe customers struggling to use our products.

Slowly, that product manager came around. We partnered to make significant improvements to our flagship product, changes that reduced costs and increased market share.

The Lesson: Make Experience Real

You won't recruit allies for UX with charts and ROI arguments alone. You must bring them into the process. You let them feel the users' pain, see the possibilities, and realize how better design can also advance their careers.

Zealotry does not convince the unconverted. Declaring UX as "obviously" important only alienates people who are measured on different outcomes. What truly changes minds is experience. When colleagues see customers struggling firsthand, when they test drive a prototype that feels dramatically better, when they realize improved design can elevate their success, that is when the value of UX becomes real to them.

Call to Action: Master the Art of UX Persuasion

Bring your partners into your UX process. Do not just report findings. Invite them to user research sessions, usability tests, and prototype reviews so they can see and feel what customers experience.

Show, don't just tell. Build quick prototypes or side-by-side comparisons of "before" and "after" experiences. Visual evidence is far more persuasive than a deck of statistics.

Connect UX improvements to performance metrics. Product managers are held accountable for financial metrics, market share, conversion rates, net promoter and customer satisfaction scores, online reviews, and several other metrics that measure product performance. Speak to what matters in their world.

Apply your empathy superpower. The most powerful message you can send when trying to convince product managers to join your UX initiatives is to state: "My job is to help *you* be more successful. How can I do that? What are your goals for your product, and let's talk about how an improved user experience can help you achieve them."

When Developers Say It Can't Be Done
Don't Automatically Take No for an Answer

I have worked with development teams at both ends of the spectrum. One team regarded every design we gave to them as a

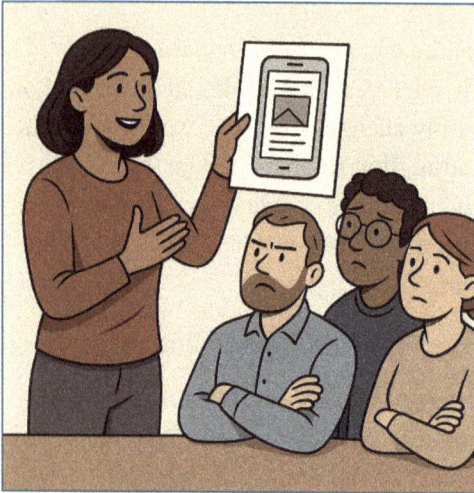

challenge. Whenever my team proposed a radical new solution to solve a persistent user problem, these developers were eager to stretch their skills and prove it could be done.

But I've also worked with teams where the answer to nearly every design proposal was a flat "no." Sometimes the excuse was technical feasibility. Other times it was time constraints. The resistance often came from junior developers who found it safer to shut down an idea than to step outside their comfort zone and try to build it.

In one role where I struggled to overcome this resistance, I had a designer on my team who was also an accomplished coder. She had decades of experience in both front-end development and design.

Whenever the developers said her proposed design was not technically feasible, she didn't argue. Instead, she sketched out some code and sent it back as a proof of concept with the message: "Yes, it can be done, and here's how."

Over time, we received less pushback from our mockups. Rather than suffer the embarrassment of being schooled by a UX designer, the developers began to see challenging designs as opportunities to learn and improve their skills.

The Lesson: When Told No, Ask for a Second Opinion

Never underestimate the value of diverse skills on a UX team. Hiring someone with a non-traditional background, or years of experience that others might overlook, can bring unique strengths to the table. In this case, one designer's coding ability helped elevate the entire team's credibility and changed the trajectory of our partnerships with development.

Looking ahead, the rise of AI will continue to blur the lines between design and development. Tools already exist that can generate the first-draft code for interfaces or workflows in minutes. This gives UX designers new leverage. If a developer dismisses an idea, designers can prototype with AI, test feasibility themselves, and bring evidence back to the table.

Call to Action: Redefine Relationships with Development

Include vibe coding in your personal development plan. Vibe coding—using AI to generate code—is a new skill that UX professionals will need to include in their annual development plans. Many free and paid training courses are available.

Challenge low-code/no-code policies. Organizations may create policies around using "out of the box" software to create new applications, arguing that it accelerates development and saves on maintenance costs down the road. However, these policies can severely restrict design options and stifle innovation. Once again, AI coding may make these policies obsolete.

Give public credit to your development teams. When a developer comes through for you on an innovative feature, shower them with accolades. Highlight this developer as an example for the entire development team to follow.

Hire for range, not just roles. Do not dismiss candidates with unconventional résumés. Sometimes the most valuable contributors are those with experience that bridges design and development.

Chapter 3: Driving Innovation

In Agile environments, UX professionals are often relegated to making relatively small, incremental improvements to existing products. We work in feature factories where we constantly try to maintain parity with our competitors. This is important work, but it's not as much fun as deeply understanding a customer's big, unmet need and solving it with an innovative, revolutionary redesign. In my view, there's no greater satisfaction than designing an experience that simplifies a human being's path to meaningful results.

Yet too often, we lose sight of that mission. We get caught up debating rounded corners, arguing about punctuation in microcopy, or perfecting the shade of a button. Those details matter, but they don't create the spark that makes a product stand out among its competitors.

In every role I've held, I've tried to step outside the job description and the product roadmap to create something different from what I've done before. Sometimes that pursuit led to breakthroughs; other times it led to failure. But it always led somewhere new.

In this chapter, I share stories of times when pushing for innovation transformed products and cultures, even when my company was content with the status quo.

UX Innovation in the Age of Agile
Working Out of Phase with Development

As someone who has practiced Human-Centered Design for decades—including its more recent incarnations like Design

Thinking and Design Sprints—I have seen design strategies come and go. These processes look good on paper, but real-world conditions rarely cooperate. The right stakeholders are unavailable. Timelines are too tight. Data is incomplete or unanalyzed. Focused multi-day sessions are interrupted by urgent matters. After a design workshop, there is a lack of follow-through. Culture and market pressure bend even the best-intentioned methods out of shape.

Then add Agile to the mix and things get very difficult. While Agile principles celebrate rapid and continuous delivery, they often gloss over the time that design iteration requires. In a two-week sprint, where developers are racing to close stories, there is little appetite for a designer showing up with new insights that disrupt velocity and burndown charts.

This pressure can push UX teams into survival mode, devolving into "mockup factories." They churn out wireframes just fast enough to stay one step ahead of development. One and done. Check the box. Move on.

But innovation is not incremental; it's a disruptive reimagining of a solution to a big, unmet customer need. Carving up design into small stories without allowing time for big-picture ideation leads to disaster. Agile champions frown on BDUF—Big Design Up

Front—as old school. But unless you have decided upon the overarching framework of a revolutionary redesign before you start building pieces of it, you end up with a fragmented, inconsistent mess that will fail in the marketplace.

That's my Innovation in the Age of Agile soapbox. Now back to our story….

After returning from a customer listening tour, I could not shake the feeling that we were sitting on a massive opportunity. The feedback I heard did more than highlight pain points. It hinted at an entirely new way our customers could engage with our flagship product.

The current product followed traditional GUI principles with a complex navigation system weaving through a maze of functionality. But my user research suggested a rethinking of this approach, one that provided a simulated view into the "users' world" with the functionality embedded into the objects in that world.

I was convinced this could be a game changer for the company. But my team was already stretched thin, focused on backlog items and roadmap commitments. Everyone was consumed with the daily grind of keeping the Agile machine running at top speed. The deep exploration, experimentation, and continuous research this idea required had no place on the schedule.

So I made a decision. If we could not pursue our innovative concept in the open, we would work on it underground—quietly, focused, and off the radar.

I pulled together a small strike team consisting of a senior designer and a prototyper. I cleared their calendars and excused them from meetings. My job was to advise and protect them from extraneous Agile noise. No distractions, just rapid iteration, constant testing, and direct contact with customers.

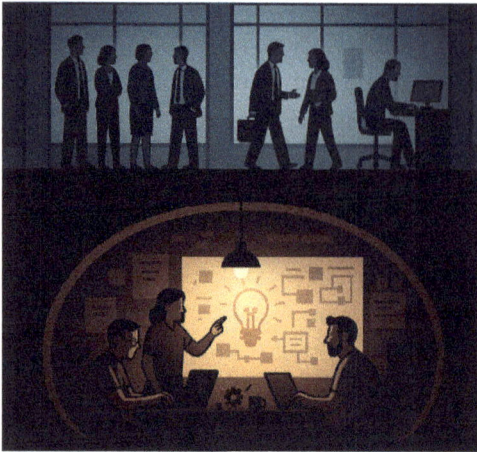

Working in that protected space, we pushed the idea far enough to make it a fully functional prototype combined with a compelling story featuring "real" characters facing real problems. Once we put it in front of executives and product partners, what had been a fragile idea became a huge opportunity that energized the entire organization.

Eventually, since we were always striving for innovation, we managed to work ourselves three months out of phase with development, giving us time to envision, research, and iterate on our next breakthrough while keeping the Agile machine at bay.

The Lesson: Innovation Requires Immersion

Innovation does not wait for a perfect slot on the roadmap or a neatly aligned set of resources. Sometimes the most transformative ideas begin in the shadows, protected from bureaucracy and nurtured by a small, focused team. Going underground is not about secrecy for its own sake. It is about creating space where fragile ideas can survive long enough to prove their worth.

Real innovation requires immersion: uninterrupted time to go deep, explore problems from every angle, challenge assumptions, and let new possibilities emerge.

Yet in most organizations today, this kind of time is nearly impossible to find. Agile has brought real benefits, but it was not designed with breakthrough innovation in mind.

Our challenge is balancing responsiveness in delivery with the need to create conditions for strategic, long-term thinking. Emerging technologies such as AI may help restore this balance.

By automating routine tasks—both for design and development—AI can expand the time available for creative exploration. It can also make it easier for developers to start from scratch when that exploration leads to genuine *"Aha!"* moments that require extensive rework.

Agile offers speed and structure for continuous delivery. But without space for thoughtful design, it risks prioritizing short-term efficiency over long-term innovation. True human-centered design requires iteration that extends beyond two-week development cycles.

Call to Action: Make Space for Breakthroughs

Schedule back-end development work before UX work. Work with the product owner to sequence sprints for back-end development first, postponing design work to later sprints to allow more time for research and iteration. Over time, you can schedule innovative UX work up to three months out of phase with development.

Start with a pilot. Once your research has revealed the need for a revolutionary redesign, choose a small part of it and work with development and product management to run a pilot. Assemble an underground team of one UXer, one product manager, and one developer. Use AI for prototyping and for coding. Allow time to throw out early concepts and code, conduct continuous research, and rapidly converge on a concept you can share with executives.

Make your pitch to leadership. When you feel you're ready to surface from the underground, prepare a bulletproof presentation and demo to the executive leadership team. Co-present with your peers in product management and development, then brace yourself for an enthusiastic reaction.

…But don't wait for permission. If you work in a company where UX maturity is very low, take the first step yourself. Do not assume leadership will support you until you've shown them your vision.

The Unique Challenges Facing In-House Consultants
The Configuration Coach That Never Launched

When I worked for a company as an in-house UX consultant, I often moved between business divisions, helping teams solve problems and improve their products. One assignment brought me into the world of medical devices.

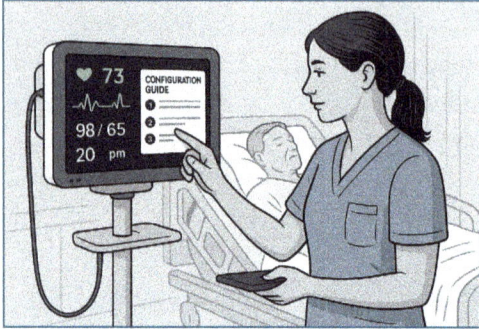

From a UX perspective, this product had a serious flaw. It was difficult to configure, easy to misconfigure, and required formal training before nurses could use it confidently. Instructions, if needed, had to be integrated into the product. If an alarm sounded and a nurse had to pause to flip through a manual, it could delay care and erode patient confidence. In healthcare, hesitation can be dangerous.

I partnered with a colleague who understood the clinical workflow in depth. Together, we built a prototype for a "configuration coach," a built-in step-by-step guide that walked nurses through setup in real time. It was discreet, fast, and designed to let them focus on patients rather than wrestle with the technology.

But as a consultant, my role was temporary. I did not have the political foothold or the long-term presence in the division to push the project forward. The idea never advanced beyond the prototype.

That experience was a reminder that in large organizations, even great ideas can fade without the right advocates to keep them alive. Sustaining innovation through to deployment requires a champion. Once the champion is gone, the project can wither from neglect.

The Lesson: Innovation Requires a Persistent Champion

In complex, high-stakes environments such as healthcare, even the best UX concepts can stall without long-term advocacy and embedded champions. Creativity and technical skills must be paired with persistence, relationship-building, and alignment with organizational priorities. Design impact depends not only on what you create, but also on your ability to navigate the politics that decide whether it survives.

Call to Action: Engage Cross-Functionally and Measure Results

Negotiate for involvement beyond delivery. If you are acting as a consultant, insist on continued engagement after the handoff. This ensures you can validate whether the solution meets its goals and can lead any necessary refinements.

Leverage internal expertise. Partner closely with internal staff who understand the product, process, and customer environment. Their deep insight provides credibility and anchors your ideas in a real-world context.

Secure stakeholder commitment early. Request dedicated time with executives, managers, and cross-functional leaders as part of the engagement. Without their attention, priorities drift and buy-in weakens.

Measure impact after delivery. Define success metrics at the start and develop a post-release assessment plan to measure the customer response to your solution. Work with salespeople, implementation specialists, trainers, and call-center agents to collect the data.

Innovation and the Corporate Immune System
My Biggest Political Mistake

When you begin driving innovation inside an organization, one of two outcomes usually follows. Colleagues join your quest because

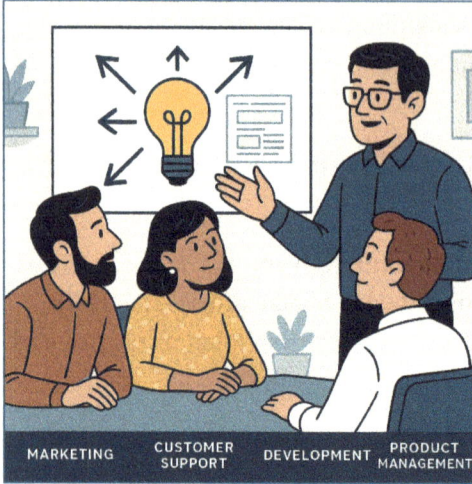

MARKETING   CUSTOMER   DEVELOPMENT   PRODUCT
             SUPPORT   MANAGEMENT

they are inspired by your energy, or the corporate immune system activates to defeat you. I have experienced both, sometimes within the same project.

Just six weeks into a new job, I pitched a bold idea directly to the leadership team. The proposal was enthusiastically received, and I left the meeting with support and encouragement to move forward. What I had not done, however, was involve peers in product management and development before presenting to leadership. From their perspective, I had bypassed them, and they were not wrong. The praise I received from leadership only deepened their irritation, and an initiative that should have united us began under a cloud of mistrust. It took months of steady work to repair those relationships.

As the project progressed, leaders from marketing, customer support, and sales began reaching out to me, eager to contribute. The initiative evolved into a true cross-functional effort and became one of the most collaborative and rewarding projects of my career. The success of the initiative demonstrated that UX was not just a design service but a strategic driver of innovation.

The Lesson: Got an Idea? Don't Go It Alone

Innovation gains momentum when colleagues are brought along from the beginning. Going it alone only fosters jealousy and resentment in the people you will need to make the project succeed.

Your goal is not to receive personal accolades for being an innovator, but to ensure the innovation survives from idea to launch. You must take care to engage your product partners early, solicit their perspectives and experience, and include them in the presentation when you propose the project to the executive leadership team.

All companies have a corporate immune system that will rise up and attack new ideas unless credit can be shared among the key partners who can make it happen.

Call to Action: Employ Revolutionary Redesign Strategies

Start small and build quietly. Begin with rough prototypes that express the essence of your idea without suggesting a finished solution. This keeps the concept flexible and open to collaboration.

Engage key product leaders early. Share your research and initial thinking with the product owner, development lead, and your direct manager. Present the idea as preliminary and tell them you need their perspectives to strengthen it.

Demonstrate value through analysis. Use research videos, UX metrics, and before-and-after comparisons to show how your concept reimagines the current experience. Your colleagues need to be inspired to join your project.

Frame the project as a shared mission. Make clear that the opportunity requires cross-functional collaboration. Position it as a collective goal, not a personal idea.

Build momentum through weekly sessions. Collaborate regularly with partners, incorporating their feedback and showing continuous progress.

Co-present to leadership. When ready, share the vision as a united cross-functional team. Present the research, the current challenges, and the prototype of the proposed redesign together.

Showcasing UX Innovation to Win Deals
Selling with Design

The best sales tool a company has is not a feature list or a clever pitch. It is UX innovation, delivered through an elegant, intuitive design.

When I first joined one organization, our flagship products were beginning to look dated. They maintained functional parity but compared to competitors, they did not reflect contemporary standards for visual design and ease of use. Customers were drifting away not because rivals had more features, but because their products looked modern, sleek, and forward-thinking. Perception mattered, and customer perception of our company was that we were not keeping up.

Refreshing the products would take a year or more, during which time our sales would continue to suffer.

Rather than wait months for a new release, we decided on a different approach. The UX team created release previews—high-fidelity prototypes of upcoming features still in development but already on the roadmap. Sales teams used these previews in demos, at industry conferences, and with prospective customers.

Initially, this made some product managers nervous. They worried about overpromising or showing features that might take longer than anticipated to make it to market. To manage the risk, we worked closely with development to ensure everything we previewed was achievable within the planned release schedule.

Along with the prototypes, we developed a script for our sales team. They now had a compelling story to tell: "Here's where we're going, and here's why staying with us is the smarter long-term choice." Customers who were on the fence about renewing began to see our company as a leading innovator in the industry.

The previews became so effective in closing deals that company leaders joked that the UX team should have its own sales quota. UX was having a visible impact on the company's balance sheet.

The Lesson: UX Innovation Advances Your Reputation

Customers buy products not only for what they do today, but also for where they appear to be headed. A preview of a visionary design can reassure hesitant customers that the company is an innovator and give sales teams a valuable tool to close deals.

But perception must rest on credibility. Overpromising erodes trust faster than any competitor can. Our previews succeeded because we collaborated closely with development to ensure every concept was technically feasible. Envisioning the future while staying grounded in reality was essential.

Release previews demonstrate that UX can be a business driver. By shaping how customers perceive your company, UX can directly influence revenue, retention, and competitiveness.

Call to Action: Position UX as a Business Driver

Show a glimpse of the future. Create high-fidelity previews that illustrate where the product is headed. Executives and customers alike want to see a vision they can believe in.

Partner with development early. Previews must be inspiring but realistic. Collaboration with engineers ensures that your future state will soon become a reality.

Equip your sales team. Provide them with prototypes and stories they can use to excite customers and close deals.

Measure business outcomes. Frame UX impact in terms of retention, renewals, and competitive wins, not just usability scores. Work with your sales team to collect data on customer acquisitions and retentions attributable to release previews.

The Accidental WOW!
Innovation Can Appear When You Least Expect It

I was preparing to attend a major industry conference where our company had secured a prime spot on the expo floor. It was a

high-stakes opportunity to showcase our latest product, which was still in development at the time, and we wanted to make a big impression. To do our part, the UX team had built an interactive prototype to highlight the upcoming product's most exciting features.

We had a card-based UI, and one feature allowed users to manually group cards by dragging and dropping them into categories. It had tested well in usability sessions, but in the fast-paced environment of an expo floor, the demo was too slow. When you have only three minutes to grab someone's attention, waiting for them to drag a handful of cards across the screen is not compelling.

So, we added a shortcut: an invisible "auto-group" button that instantly sorted the cards using animation. It was not on the roadmap. It was not even intended for the real product. We added it to the prototype only to keep the demo moving.

Then something unexpected happened. The first time we pressed that button during a live demo, people lit up. "WOW!" they exclaimed. It sorts the cards for me automatically? That would save me so much time!" They could not contain their excitement.

What we had created as a demo convenience turned out to be the feature customers wanted most. When we returned from the conference, the idea moved from a "demo trick" to a development priority. The engineers accepted the challenge, and it went on to become one of the product's standout features.

The Lesson: Sometimes Innovation Arrives Unexpectedly

Innovation does not always come from meticulously planned roadmaps or carefully researched features. Sometimes it emerges from the unplanned, the improvised, even the accidental. The "auto-group" button was never intended to be more than a demo accelerator. In the hands of real people, under real conditions, it revealed itself as a breakthrough.

Call to Action: Act on Tangential Inspiration

Watch for excited reactions. Pay attention to the unfiltered responses of customers, stakeholders, and colleagues. Genuine surprise or delight often reveals a game-changing feature that could stand out among your competitors.

Treat serendipity as data. If an improvised feature excites people, don't dismiss it just because it was not part of the plan. Capture the reaction and consider how it might inform the real product.

Tell the story with live experiences. Nothing compares to the impact of letting people see and feel how a feature could make a difference in their lives. When demoing features, set the context of use with a real-world story that customers can relate to.

Record the excitement. The accidental WOW! might be a challenge to develop, but the response from customers shows that the effort will be well worth it. To prove the potential ROI to your colleagues and executives, record their reactions and gather testimonials describing how the feature would elevate the product above the competition.

The Take-Away Method
Breaking Current Patterns to Find Breakthroughs

One of the simplest but most powerful techniques I have used to unlock breakthrough thinking is taking away the design patterns you have come to rely on, the ones you accept as "just the way

things are." Only then can you create the space for something radically new.

Here's how I run the exercise.

First, we model the current experience for achieving a very specific result. In my workshops, I would choose an everyday example such as "changing the color of a wall." It's important to phrase the task in generic terms, e.g., *change* the color of a wall, not *paint* a wall. If I said paint, we'd bias ourselves toward a particular solution.

Next, we map out every action that is currently required to achieve the result, the information needed to perform each action, and the object in the human–product system that owns the responsibility for performing each action and providing each bit of information.

Finally, take away one or more of the responsibilities assigned to the human component in the system. For example, what happens if the user is no longer responsible for dipping a brush into a paint can and applying it to the wall? How can we change the color of the wall if that assumption is stripped away?

That's the challenge I give to design teams: imagine you can't use tabs, dropdown menus, or toolbars in your interface. If those patterns are taken away, how would you design the system then?

If the user does not transfer the color to the wall, maybe the wall object itself changes color. Or maybe we consider another object that can transport the paint to the wall. We can now imagine new solutions that seem impossible today but could become commonplace tomorrow.

The key is not to discount an idea simply because it feels unrealistic in the present. Every breakthrough product we use once seemed impossible. To innovate, we must challenge assumptions, reassign responsibilities, and imagine solutions that seem impossible only because we haven't challenged ourselves to think beyond the present.

The Lesson: Question Your Unquestioned Assumptions

Innovation comes from questioning the assumptions that we believe are inviolable. The simple act of stripping away "the way it has always been done" forces us to think differently. When you remove a user's responsibility for performing an action or supplying information, you are forced to find another way.

By challenging assumptions, redistributing responsibilities, and refusing to accept the status quo, you uncover possibilities that ordinary iteration would never reveal.

Call to Action: Eliminate Reliance on Design "Crutches"

Challenge assumptions deliberately. In your next project, identify one or two "givens" about how users interact with your product and ask what would happen if this responsibility shifted elsewhere.

Use language carefully. Frame your problem statements without bias toward current solutions. Keep them outcome-focused so that new ideas can emerge naturally.

Reassign responsibility. Ask what would happen if the user did not have to complete a specific step. Imagine whether the product, the environment, or another component in the system could take it on instead.

UX Research Labs to Envision the Future
The Disappearing Space for Innovation

One of the most frustrating parts of my career has been watching breakthrough ideas slip away because I could not find the time and space to shepherd them through to completion.

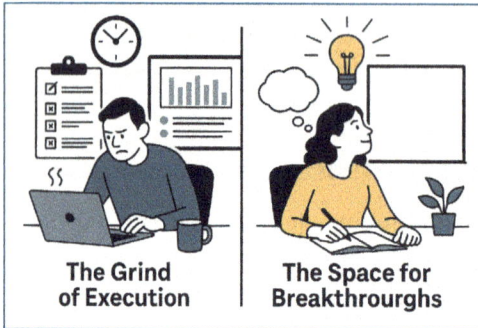

The Grind of Execution | The Space for Breakthrourghs

At one company, I pursued what I believed could be a game-changing mindset, model, and methodology for reimagining the customer experience. If implemented, I was convinced it would have positioned our products light-years beyond our competitors.

I captured research findings, early concepts, and rough frameworks in a PowerPoint deck. What began as a handful of slides eventually ballooned into more than a hundred. Each slide represented a fragment of a larger vision: how we could redesign our systems with human-product collaboration at the core.

But no one wants to sit through a 100-slide manifesto, and I couldn't carve out time in my schedule to translate the depth of my thought experiment into a narrative that others could absorb. I would get close to a breakthrough, then the daily demands of sprints, deadlines, and fire drills would pull me away. After a few months, when I could finally get back to my ideas, I had lost the thread and had to start over again.

I know I left dozens of innovative solutions to unmet customer needs behind simply because I failed to navigate the politics of time and priorities.

Today, innovation is a side pursuit. Instead of expecting breakthrough thinking to emerge in the gaps between back-to-back meetings, organizations should invest in UX Research Labs—

dedicated spaces where senior design fellows can focus on the next horizon. The payoff would be true disruptive innovations that could redefine industries. But alas, the modern company's obsession with shareholder value and continuous delivery offer no room on the balance sheet for investments without guaranteed deliverables and results.

The Lesson: Take Time Away from Delivery to Think

Expecting breakthrough thinking to emerge only in stolen moments between Agile sprints and deadlines is unrealistic. Organizations that create dedicated labs, appoint senior fellows, and protect exploratory work are the ones most likely to leapfrog competitors. Innovation should not be a side project. It is the engine of long-term success.

Call to Action: Protect Space for Breakthroughs

Go deep, then resurface. Distill your thinking into a clear, compelling story others can absorb in minutes. A breakthrough idea that can't be communicated simply will not gain traction.

Fight for protected time. Block space for exploration and defend it as fiercely as any deliverable. If you do not protect it, execution will always consume it.

Build allies early. Share fragments of your vision with trusted colleagues. Invite them into the process so the idea becomes a shared effort. Meet weekly to keep momentum going.

Anchor innovation to business stakes. Tie your vision to metrics leaders care about: cost savings, revenue growth, customer retention, and competitiveness. Frame it as essential, not optional.

Push for institutional space. Advocate for UX research labs, innovation fellowships, and protected innovation sprints. Position them as necessities for the long-term viability of your company.

Researching, Thinking, Experimenting, Teaching
The Disappearing Space for Innovation

The best role I ever had was on the Design for the User (DFU) team, a centralized group of internal UX consultants. It was the

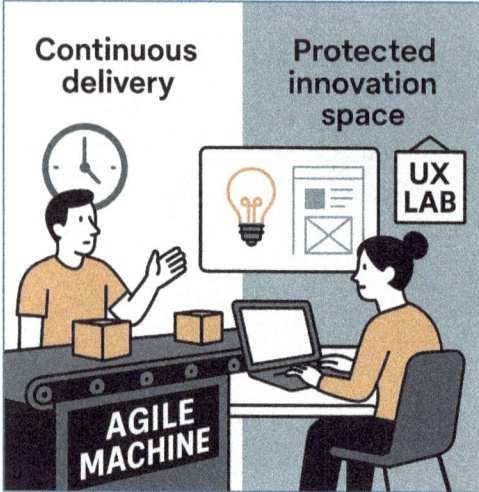

closest thing I have seen to a true UX think tank inside a corporation. We had the freedom to step back, study the bigger picture, and challenge how our products were conceived, developed, and delivered.

I doubt I will ever see a job like that again.

Today, UX as a profession feels like it is in retreat. Fewer companies are investing in creative customer experiences, even though the need has never been greater. As I said in Chapter 2, I will never forget when a product manager told me: "As long as we're no worse than our competitors, we really have no incentive to invest in UX." That kind of thinking does not push anyone forward. It locks organizations into a race to the bottom.

These labs—those rare, protected spaces where teams once explored bold new ideas without the pressure of immediate ROI—have mostly disappeared. R&D has, in many places, devolved into just "D." Agile may accelerate delivery, but it has also made it harder to carve out time for deeper research, reflection, or true innovation.

Even "Passion Project Fridays" get swallowed by deadlines, bug fixes, or the next sprint review. Internal teams are left trying to sustain change in an environment designed for output, not for breakthrough thinking.

I have worked on my share of visionary concepts, but I often wonder if that kind of work is even possible in today's shareholder-first culture. Innovation requires patience, focus, and a willingness to let people explore ideas that may not pay off right away. Those are exactly the things most organizations are unwilling to fund.

The Lesson: Safeguarding Innovation

The Design for the User team remains one of the most vivid reminders of what's possible when organizations protect time and space for innovation. But the corporate landscape has shifted. Agile and shareholder-first priorities have left little room for experimentation. What has been lost is not just the luxury of exploration, but the discipline of envisioning what comes next. Without that balance, organizations risk becoming efficient at delivering the wrong things.

Innovation will not survive on passion alone. You can't expect after-hours tinkering or "Passion Project Fridays" to produce the kind of leaps forward that labs once nurtured. Organizations must be intentional. They must carve out protected time, fund exploratory work, and measure its impact differently from how they measure an Agile sprint.

Call to Action: Ask Your Team to Propose Innovations

Rotational innovation. Setting aside resources and budget to stand up a formal innovation lab is probably not feasible in your company. But try to do this as a starting point:

Ask members of your UX team to propose a revolutionary redesign of one of your products. From their submissions, choose one project and give the creator three months to do the research, show a prototype, and pitch the business case. If it is approved by leadership and becomes a funded project, rotate the designer off the innovation phase to lead the development cycle and see the project through to delivery and metrics collection. Then rotate the next project and its inventor into the next three-month innovation phase. Repeat.

Failure to Follow Through
The Brilliant Ideas That Got Away

Over the years, I've organized periodic "design jams" where we would step away from the daily grind and focus entirely on one of those wicked-hard design problems that had been haunting our legacy product. Our goal was to formulate bold, transformative solutions that could redefine the user experience and give us a competitive edge.

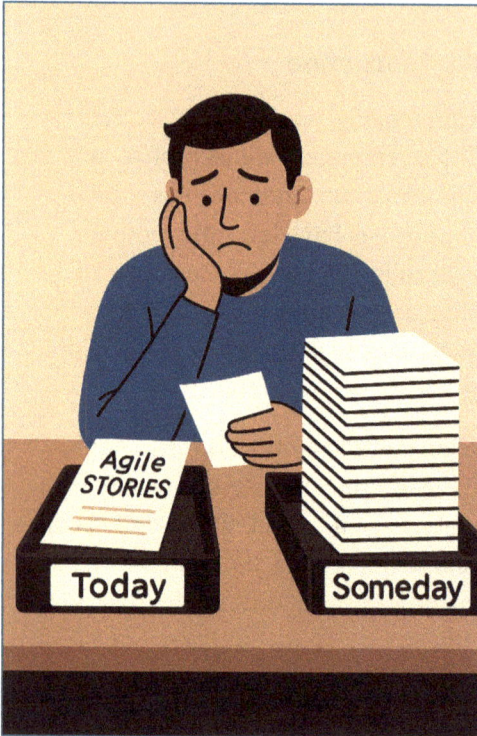

By the end of each design jam, a handful of promising concepts would rise to the top, and, more often than not, we would leave with a clear path forward. I left the room with the hope that we could keep the momentum going in the weeks and months to come.

But, when we returned to our desks, reality intervened. The Agile machine demanded feeding. Sprint planning filled our calendars. Urgent requests from stakeholders drowned out our long-term vision. The ideas we had been so energized about faded. Most never made it past the concept stage.

The Lesson: Innovation Requires Follow-Through

The hardest part of innovation is not coming up with bold ideas. The hard part is keeping them alive long enough to make a difference. Breakthrough thinking can emerge when teams are freed from the noise of daily work. But without protection, those sparks fade under the weight of urgent tasks and sprint cycles.

Call to Action: Try to Balance Innovation with Delivery

Protect dedicated time for innovation. Block calendar time, weekly or monthly, for design jams, concept refinement, or prototyping. Treat this time as non-negotiable, the same way you would treat a retrospective or a design review.

Create a system for idea follow-through. Document every promising idea in a UX-proprietary backlog and assign owners to shepherd them forward. Iteration on lightweight prototypes can keep momentum alive until the right opportunity to reveal the idea arrives.

Balance short-term delivery with long-term vision. Agile prioritizes speed and iteration, but don't confuse "fast" with "finished." Advocate for cycles of deep exploration alongside your sprints. Try to convince stakeholders that breakthrough innovation requires some degree of freedom from the daily grind.

Build accountability into the process. When your team commits to pursuing a promising idea, tie it to timeboxed milestones: who will prototype, who will gather validation data, and who will present to leadership. Include these activities in your OKRs.

Learn from the backlog of unrealized ideas. Your "graveyard" of unfinished ideas is a resource, not a failure. Periodically revisit it. You may find solutions that were not feasible two years ago but are now perfectly aligned with new technology or market needs.

Disruptive Service Design
Pushing Back on the Business of Dark Patterns

Lately, there has been a lot of talk in the UX community about dark patterns, but not all dark patterns appear in products.

Sometimes they are buried in company policies and business models in an effort to profit from customer mistakes.

I mentioned earlier that a support manager once told me that our company should not make our products *too* simple because we generated a lot of revenue from support contracts. In his opinion, customer frustration should be baked into the business model.

The story of Blockbuster Video is a prime example of how a dark pattern brought down a company. Although I never worked for Blockbuster, I was a frequent victim of their policies. My teenage son would go to Blockbuster every week to pick out movies. And every week I would get a surprise notice of late fees for movies I didn't even know he had checked out. I was paying more in late fees than in rental fees.

Banking on customer mistakes was integral to Blockbuster's business model, but it left them vulnerable to new competitors. Netflix came along with a mail-order service that allowed customers to keep movies as long as they pleased—without late fees, a policy that disrupted the industry, and Blockbuster eventually went bankrupt. (Maybe Netflix used the Take-Away Method described earlier in this chapter.)

The Lesson: Advocate Against Evil

When revenue depends on customer mistakes, frustration, or confusion, the company may think it has created a dependable income stream. In reality, it has created a massive opportunity for competitors.

UX professionals must expand our definition of experience design beyond screens and workflows. Deceptive policy, pricing, or service models are part of the user experience, and they demand the same scrutiny as any other aspect of interaction design. We must have the courage to call these issues out to product managers and executives. Short-term profits may cloud leadership's judgment, but history shows that companies who profit from pain points eventually pay the price.

Ethical business policies are a competitive advantage. Designing for simplicity is not just the right thing to do—it's often the thing that keeps the business competitive.

Call to Action: Design Policies as Well as Products

Expand your scope of design. Do not limit your definition of UX to screens and workflows. Look at policies and business practices as part of the end-to-end experience. Consider yourself a business owner and act accordingly.

Call out hidden dark patterns. When you see revenue being driven by customer mistakes, confusion, or complexity, speak up. These patterns may look profitable today, but they erode customer loyalty over time.

Tell cautionary stories. Use examples like Blockbuster, which built its revenue model on late fees only to be displaced by Netflix. Share stories of other companies that lost market dominance by exploiting customers. Show that there is a business vulnerability inherent in being "evil."

Frame dark patterns in business terms. Translate customer frustration into metrics leadership cares about: churn, support costs, Net Promoter Score, or market share. Make the case that simplicity and fairness are not just ethical, they are strategic.

Going Back to the Drawing Board
Rediscovering the Essence of UX

When I immersed myself in the broader world of UX by reading research, following thought leaders, and studying new

methodologies, I came to realize that most frameworks were solid in theory, but many did not survive inside my company's environment of tight schedules and resource constraints.

So, I stepped back and asked a deceptively simple question: What problem are we really trying to solve with UX?

The answer is not about usability in the academic sense. Our real challenge is finding ways to deliver on the promise our companies make to their customers. When someone buys our product, they aren't paying for features. They're paying for outcomes, or as I framed it back then, they are paying for results. At its essence, UX should have a singular focus on removing every barrier that stands between people and their outcomes. And for the stubborn barriers we cannot remove right away, we must provide information and support at the right time, in the right place, and in the right form so customers have a chance to succeed in spite of vestigial complexity.

In the 1990s, I codified that approach into a two-day course and began teaching it to product teams around the world. It was practical, non-technical, and designed for engineering-driven environments. Teams embraced it. Products improved. And customers noticed the difference.

But I also learned something important. No model is ever final. Every field of study must evolve. There is always more to refine, revise, discard, and invent as technology advances and customer expectations shift. We need innovation not just in our products and services, but in the practice of UX.

That's where you come in.

The Lesson: You Are the Future of UX

Progress comes from asking new questions, pushing deeper into the practice, and exploring new intersections between design, technology, and human behavior.

We need the next generation of designers, researchers, writers, and strategists to challenge the boundaries of what UX is supposed to be. We need fresh eyes on old problems and the courage to imagine solutions that no one has yet tried.

Like other veterans in the field, I have done my part in laying some of the groundwork. But the future of UX does not belong to me. Our field can evolve only if we make space for the next generation to question and reimagine today's "best practices."

Call to Action: Reinvent UX

Ask bigger questions. Don't stop at applying existing frameworks and methods. Step back and ask what problem UX is trying to solve and whether your current approach is really solving it.

Teach what you know. Share your models and methods, whether in a course, at a conference, or in an informal brown-bag session. Teaching deepens your own understanding; challenges from your audience inspire you to rethink what you know.

Refine continuously. Treat every framework as a living system. Adapt it as technology evolves and as customer expectations shift.

Be the future of UX. Don't wait for permission to challenge the status quo. Experiment with bold ideas and invite others to join you. The next chapter of UX depends on those willing to question past assumptions and strike out to find new ground.

Chapter 4: Leadership Challenges

As you read the following vignettes, it may seem that my experiences with executive leadership are predominantly negative, but that is not the case. If things are going well, you don't need to tell as many stories and learn as many lessons as when leadership places roadblocks in your career.

I've had many great bosses in my career. I tend to believe that the people I work with have good intentions. We may have disagreements, but those disagreements are born out of a genuine desire to do the right thing for our customers. I understand the pressures company leaders are under when they are held accountable for results that may be out of their control.

But I have reported to managers who were at best inept, and at worst were malignant narcissists. I've tried to get along with everyone and in most cases I could, but occasionally I found myself in an untenable position with a manager whose only interest was self-promotion.

In this chapter, I share stories from both sides of that spectrum: lessons learned from leaders who inspired me and from those who nearly derailed me. Some situations called for finding common ground, aligning around shared values, and helping move a leadership agenda forward. Others required recognizing when the healthiest choice was to walk away, whether by my choice or theirs.

Speaking Truth to Power
Establishing Trust Before Telling the Truth

Our job is not to share opinions, but to deliver conclusions grounded in research, domain knowledge, and data. Yet even the

best conclusions will encounter resistance if credibility has not been established first.

Shortly after starting a new job, I was eager to prove myself as a user experience expert. I went directly to senior leadership with a pointed critique of the product. My analysis was accurate, but I had not taken time to understand the constraints the team had faced, the deadlines they worked under, or the trade-offs they had been forced to make leading up to the current design. Without that context, my analysis landed as criticism rather than recommendations. Instead of generating excitement for a better future state, they triggered defensiveness.

I learned from this mistake and took a different approach in my next role. I asked the CPO which of our many products was most in need of a user experience overhaul. When I got the answer, I observed users, documented pain points, and identified areas of improvement. But I did not present everything at once. Instead, I suggested we start with small, achievable fixes. The team implemented them, and customers responded positively. Each small success built trust and credibility with the leadership team.

Over the next six months, I continued releasing recommendations gradually. Each round of improvements demonstrated the value of UX and strengthened my relationship with the product team. By the time the CPO asked for my candid opinion of the state of the product, we had developed a strong partnership.

This time I didn't hold back. Despite the incremental enhancements we had made, I told him the overall user experience sucked. The product needed a complete redesign if it was to remain competitive into the future. Because I had established my credibility, my honesty was met with appreciation, not defensiveness. Together, we launched efforts that transformed the product into a leader in its industry.

The Lesson: Trust Before Truth

Credibility is the foundation of influence in UX. Even the strongest analysis will fail if shared before trust has been built. By starting small, demonstrating results, and building relationships gradually, you create the conditions for candor. Once credibility is established, blunt assessments can be shared constructively and lead to meaningful change. UX leadership is not only about having the right answers, but also about knowing when and how to share them.

Call to Action: Build Your Reputation for Collaboration

Start with quick wins. Your research has undoubtedly revealed some small design changes that have the potential to deliver impactful results. It could be a label change or just surfacing a common task that is currently buried in the navigation taxonomy. Choose one of these to work on first, then measure its impact.

Work with your call center team. Support costs are always an executive pain point. Ask the call center manager to provide you with monthly statistics for the top ten most frequent support calls. Find calls that are due to "user misunderstandings" and formulate design solutions. Measure the drop in calls after your solution is deployed and use this success story to build your credibility.

Invest time in relationships. Build trust with product managers, developers, and leaders by demonstrating that you are advocating for their success as well as for your users'. Recognize that trust and influence accrue gradually. Once established, they enable you to advocate for more ambitious, transformational change.

Getting Shut Out of the Room
When UX Perspective Is Perceived as Troublemaking

Some of the most critical product decisions are made long before a designer is asked to create a wireframe. If UX is not represented in those conversations, design gets reduced to an afterthought—the dreaded "just make it pretty" directive that we all hate to receive.

I've experienced this more than once. At one company, I discovered that epics were being written, stories crafted, and roadmaps drawn up without a single UX voice in the room. The new VP of Product, someone who neither understood nor trusted UX, had decided our role was execution rather than direction. We were not part of her inner circle, and so we were sidelined.

In another case, the exclusion was more subtle but just as deliberate. A senior leader did not say it outright, but the reason he excluded me from a task force he was leading was because my perspective might challenge his authority or derail the approach he had already chosen. My expertise was not viewed as a contribution. It was viewed as a threat.

The costs of my exclusion showed up quickly. Beautiful PowerPoint decks were created for presentations to executives, but opportunities for simpler, more elegant solutions were bypassed. By the time UX was invited in, it was too late. Challenging decisions came across as undermining work that was already done.

I don't believe these leaders excluded UX because they thought it lacked value. They excluded us because they feared our influence.

When you come armed with customer knowledge, grounded research, and the ability to visualize new possibilities, you bring power into the room. And power can make people uneasy.

The Lesson: Build Relationships with the Power Brokers

UX does not just need a *seat* at the table, it needs *allies* at the table. If we come across as disruptors, we will be treated as outsiders. But if we show up as partners, making it clear that our goal is to help the team succeed, we stand a far better chance of shaping the conversation before foundational decisions are made.

When we make it clear that our goal is collaboration rather than self-promotion, we have a much better chance of being invited to key meetings. It's more important to let others share the credit for our contributions than to demand all the credit for ourselves.

Call to Action: Make Your Perspective Indispensable

Use your boss as leverage. Ask your boss to reach out to the meeting organizer and request that you be invited to all product planning meetings. This approach could cause some resentment, but once you're in the meetings, you can use diplomacy to demonstrate your willingness to collaborate.

Build one-on-one relationships. Schedule conversations with product management and development leaders. Ask where UX can support their priorities and position yourself as an enabler of their goals.

Support those who exclude you. If a leader shuts you out, don't escalate the conflict. Instead, provide them with something useful like insights, visuals, or data they can share at the next meeting. Eventually, they will invite you to a meeting to explain your ideas to the rest of the team. Even if you're not part of the inner circle, you'll be perceived as a valuable adviser.

Meet with the meeting organizer. After each meeting, drop by the leader's desk to ask how the meeting went. Keep it informal, but volunteer to help with an action item if you have something to contribute.

The Perils of Changes in Executive Leadership
The Missed Opportunity with TCE

There was a time in my career when I was well known across the company for championing UX maturity. I had built a reputation as

both an expert and a trusted partner, someone who could translate UX principles into pragmatic solutions and understood the very real scheduling and resource constraints our product teams faced. I traveled around the world, teaching classes, consulting on projects, and helping divisions integrate user experience practices into their processes. It was demanding work, but deeply rewarding.

Then came a new CEO. For the first time in the company's history, the board looked beyond its internal talent to hire someone from the outside. She arrived with energy, bold ideas, and a signature initiative called the Total Customer Experience, or TCE. In today's language, we would call it service design or an end-to-end customer experience initiative: mapping and improving every step of a customer's journey from product research to purchase to use to support to obsolescence and replacement.

I thought this was my chance to deeply embed UX into the company's culture. Given my reputation, my reach across divisions, and my credibility with both engineers and product managers, I assumed I would play a central role in shaping and implementing TCE.

I was wrong.

The new CEO had not come to listen. She came with her own playbook. The entire TCE process arrived pre-packaged in a deck of PowerPoint slides. It looked polished, but had little substance. What's more, the managers who stepped forward to implement the initiative weren't seasoned UX practitioners. They were leaders skilled in management politics, eager to align themselves with the CEO's agenda despite their lack of experience in human-centered design.

Within a year, my role had been sidelined. My consulting team dissolved when executive sponsorship disappeared. I was reassigned to a small training group where I continued teaching workshops, mainly because they generated revenue. My influence evaporated, and eventually I moved to a smaller product division before volunteering for a downsizing incentive.

The Lesson: New Leadership Means Starting Over

When leadership changes, you can't rely on past reputation alone. You have to reintroduce yourself, restate your value, and claim your seat at the table before someone else does.

New leaders may marginalize those who are admired, powerful, or have their own popular vision. They may see you less as a partner and more as a rival. Never assume that being "known" is enough. Every leadership transition is a reset.

Call to Action: Help the New Leader Succeed

Introduce yourself to the new leader. Don't assume your reputation will speak for itself. Schedule time with the new leader, ask about their philosophy and plans, introduce your perspective, and show how your work can support their agenda.

Listen first, position second. Approach new leadership with curiosity. Ask about their vision, goals, and challenges. Then frame your contributions as enablers of their success, not as competing priorities. Recast your UX initiatives in ways that directly connect to their terminology, their strategy, and their metrics, but don't sacrifice your integrity.

Surviving Incompetent Leadership
Hint: You Probably Can't

There are three kinds of UX bosses.

The first kind are the champions. They are experienced UX

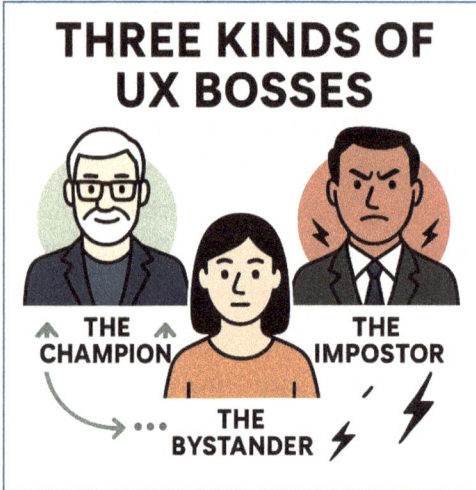

THREE KINDS OF
UX BOSSES

THE CHAMPION

THE IMPOSTOR

THE BYSTANDER

veterans who truly understand what you do and how you do it. They advocate for your ideas, shield you from unnecessary battles, and make sure your team has the resources to thrive.

The second kind of boss freely admits they don't know much about UX but they trust you to know your craft. They support your efforts, and most importantly, stay out of your way. This arrangement often works just fine.

Then there is the dangerous kind. These are the managers who don't understand UX but because they are on the management career fast track, they have been handed responsibility for your team anyway. They pretend to know more than they do, insert themselves where they shouldn't, and in the worst cases, actively undermine your work.

I've reported to all three types. The first two I could work with. The third is where things became untenable.

When my team was reassigned to a new "type three" manager, he called me in for an introductory meeting. His message was simple: "I just want everyone on my team to be happy!" (He actually said that.) That sounded fine on the surface, but in the coming weeks it became clear that he had no idea how to lead a UX practice.

A few months later, while visiting our UX contingent in India, he hired two new designers without telling me or even informing my on-site UX manager. There were no open requisitions; they just showed up one morning and said they had been hired by our boss.

Soon after, during a one-on-one, he asked me for a list of UX conferences he could attend. But he didn't just want to attend and learn; he wanted to speak. It seems after a few months, he believed he had acquired the wisdom of an experienced UX professional and was ready to share it with the broader UX community. His actual motivation? Promoting his personal "eminence" within the company and the industry to advance his career.

And then came the real blow. One morning, without warning, he laid off the entire U.S. contingent of the UX team, all thirteen of us. Managers, designers, and researchers were all gone in a single day. He left only the India team to somehow carry on with half the staff. My best guess is that he got credit for cutting costs and earned kudos from senior leadership for "right-sizing" the organization.

It was the worst experience of my career leading UX teams. Not because we lost good people, but because we lost them for all the wrong reasons: ignorance, ego, and self-promotion.

The Lesson: Some Things Are Beyond Your Control

Not every boss is equipped to lead a UX team. Some empower, some trust, and some undermine. When you find yourself reporting to the third type—the ones who don't understand UX but feel the need to control it—you are in dangerous territory.

Short-term cost-cutting will always be prioritized over UX when short-sighted leadership is in charge. The best team, with the best talent, can still be dismantled if its value is not understood, or worse, if it is seen as a political threat.

Call to Action: Run!

Start looking for another job. It's very unlikely that you can successfully work with a borderline sociopath. Yes, they do exist.

When New Reporting Relationships Don't Work
No-Win Relationships with New Bosses

At none of the companies I worked for was there ever a Chief Experience Officer or even an executive role solely dedicated to

UX. Instead, the UX function was passed from VP to VP. Sometimes we reported to development, sometimes to marketing, sometimes to product management. Any of these structures can work if the leader values UX and understands its role. But in my experience, the best results came when UX reported to the CTO. At least there, the connection between designing things and building things gave our work some traction.

The challenge came whenever the department was handed off. Each new leader had to be retrained, brought up to speed on what UX really does, what it contributes, and why it matters. Some were open to learning about UX, others not so much.

One case in particular stands out. A newly hired VP was given oversight of several functions, including UX. His expertise was elsewhere, and it showed. He didn't speak the language of UX, didn't ask questions about it, and wasn't interested in learning.

His very first assignment revealed the disconnect. He asked all his direct reports to propose five to seven strategic initiatives for the company to pursue. I drew from our user research and proposed bold initiatives for increasing user engagement, creating evidence-based dashboards, developing a decision console to empower customers, and fostering better cross-department collaboration. These were real problems that could move the business forward if we solved them.

But my proposals were not just ignored—they were completely out of sync with the agenda he already had in mind. What he wanted was superficial business-speak, polished soundbites that looked good in a slide deck. What I gave him were tough, meaningful problems to solve.

It became clear that UX was never going to be on his agenda. When I was laid off a few months later, his words to me were, "You haven't done anything wrong." Not long after, most of my UX team resigned. A few months after that, he was gone, too.

The Lesson: Some Problems Have No Solution

When leadership changes, you can't rely on past reputation alone. A new boss does not inherit your history, your influence, or your allies. In fact, the very visibility and credibility you have built may be seen as a threat.

There are no-win relationships with certain managers. If UX doesn't fit neatly into their agenda, they will ignore, sideline, or even lay you off. No amount of evidence or passion can overcome a leader who simply doesn't grok UX. Sometimes the system corrects itself, but not always in time to save you. The question is whether you can outlast them or they will outlast you.

Call to Action: Do Your Best, But Prepare to Exit

Gauge the new leader's unspoken agenda. Meet with the new leader immediately, tell your story, and ask how UX can support their goals. Listen closely and observe their body language. They may have favorites among their direct reports and it may become clear that you are not one of them.

Know when to move on. If, after several attempts, you don't speak the same language as your new boss and cannot find common ground, you're probably in a no-win relationship. Remember, it's not about you. Sometimes the wisest decision is to prepare for your next opportunity.

Your Bosses are Jealous of You
When Too Much Success Is Dangerous

One of the double-edged swords of being a UX professional is visibility. We are often highly visible within organizations, especially smaller ones, because of our talent for visualizing compelling solutions to design problems. We are also good at navigating politics: recruiting allies and showing others how UX can directly advance their success.

That visibility can make you popular and powerful. But it can also make you a target.

I once worked for a manager who truly valued UX. He trusted me to lead a talented team of designers, managers, and visual specialists, and together we produced strong customer outcomes. But his boss saw things differently. For reasons I never fully understood, my influence and visibility must have threatened his own stature within the company.

My manager asked me to design a course on UX that would be mandatory training for the entire organization. The objective of the course was to help everyone understand how UX worked and how they could participate in the process. Before rolling it out, I presented a pilot to the executive leadership team to get their feedback and approval.

The response was overwhelmingly positive, except for my boss's boss. He made offhanded remarks suggesting the material was gimmicky, filled with props and fake principles. Still, we launched the course, and employees enjoyed it. The evaluations always received high scores.

But behind the scenes, my increased exposure seemed only to deepen this executive's suspicion. Major projects that would normally have gone to my team were instead farmed out to contractors. Eventually, I was reassigned to a new manager who had little understanding of the value UX could bring.

I stayed as long as I could, partly because I needed the income, but mostly to protect my team from the dysfunction swirling above us. But in the end, my entire team and I were laid off in a single day. All it took was one leader with enough power and insecurity to dismantle the UX organization we had worked so hard to build.

The Lesson: Executives Can View You as a Competitor

When you have built credibility, earned influence, and inspired others, you become highly visible. New leaders, especially those eager to establish themselves, may see your visibility as a threat.

When jealousy lives in your direct chain of command, it can be a no-win situation. You can do everything right—deliver results, build alliances, share credit—and still find yourself sidelined because your influence threatens someone else's personal brand.

Call to Action: Try Your Best, Then Move On

Reintroduce yourself with every leadership change. Schedule time with new leaders to share your perspective, highlight your team's impact, and ask how you can support their vision.

Frame your work in their language. Translate UX outcomes into the metrics and priorities that matter most to leadership.

Share credit generously. Jealous leaders often feel threatened when others get the spotlight. Share credit openly with leaders, peers, and cross-functional partners so that you are seen as someone who elevates others.

Know when to move on. Sometimes the best option is to take your talent to a place where it will be appreciated, not stifled.

Escaping a Toxic Company Culture
The Questions I Should Have Asked

At one company, I went through one of the most grueling interview processes of my career. Over six weeks, I met with at

least seven different managers before finally being offered the job. It felt like a victory at the time, but within a year, every single one of those managers who had interviewed me was either laid off or fired, including my boss.

There were pockets of innovation and bright spots of employee-centered leadership. But overall, the culture was toxic. The signs were there when I interviewed; I just didn't recognize them soon enough.

When I was hired, the company treated me like an executive. They paid for my relocation through a top-tier executive moving firm. They even promised me an office—a real office and not a cubicle—which I had never had before. Months went by, though, and the office never materialized even though there was vacant space and other new hires got theirs. This should have been a signal that UX was not valued as highly as other corporate functions.

About once a month, I was invited to the executive leadership meetings in the secluded wing where the CEO and EVPs kept their offices. Those meetings were tense, combative, and joyless. It was there that I first heard whispers of "Bloody October," the company's annual ritual of mass layoffs. Employees were numerically ranked against one another on a scorecard, and every October the lowest-scoring people were cut.

I left as soon as I had another opportunity. But looking back, I should have asked better questions during the hiring process. Simple questions like: How long have you been with the company? How stable is the leadership team? What is the turnover like here? The answers would have revealed what was coming.

The Lesson: Look for Signs of Toxicity When You Interview

When leadership changes, or when you join a new organization, you can't rely on first impressions or the company's past reputation alone. Culture reveals itself in the small details, and it's your job to notice them.

Perks like relocation packages and offices may look like signs of respect, but they can also mask deeper problems. Watch closely for signs of toxicity, like if the executive leadership team is sequestered and inaccessible, who gets access to whom, the tenor of all-hands meetings, and the attrition rate of senior leaders. Those patterns tell you more than company websites ever will.

Call to Action: Ask Questions & Notice Behaviors

Ask tenure questions in interviews. Do not just focus on the role. Ask each interviewer how long they have been with the company and what changes they have seen. High turnover is a red flag.

Probe culture beyond the surface. Ask about leadership style, how decisions are made, and how teams handle conflict.

Observe signals of value. Notice how your function is treated compared to others. Is UX given the same respect as engineering, product management, or marketing?

Watch for power rituals. Who sits where, who gets offices, and how leaders speak in meetings are all indicators of hierarchy and culture. Are meetings collegial or combative? And though it might sound simple, are people smiling or tense?

Protect yourself with options. Even if you step into a toxic culture, you are not trapped. Keep your network alive and be ready to move when you see the writing on the wall.

Proposing Initiatives to Executive Leadership
Facing the Power Room

I have had several chances to sit across the table from senior leaders, the VPs and above who could either champion a UX

initiative or quietly kill it. These meetings were high stakes and carried the potential to move UX into a greater position of influence, but they were also kind of scary.

Early in my career, I was lucky to be working in an egalitarian culture. When I reached out to the VP of my division for a meeting, he said yes without hesitation. When I launched into my demo, naturally, the computer crashed. But I pressed on, talking him through the initiative I had been pursuing on my own time.

He listened politely, thanked me for my effort, and told me to come back once I had more data to support the proposal. At the time, I walked away deflated, but years later, I understood his response differently. Senior leaders juggle an endless stream of proposals. They can't chase every one, no matter how promising. Data was not a delay tactic; it was the price of entry.

Later in my career, I was invited to present at a senior leadership offsite, a much bigger stage. My team and I had a vision for how our product's experience could evolve, backed by research and illustrated with mockups and a story. We had worked for months, but because of sprint demands, much of the vision work was done in scraps of leftover time.

When the day came, I stood in front of the company's power brokers and shared our story. They listened. They nodded. They thanked me. And then nothing. The presentation had been polite theater, but not a catalyst for change. I squandered the opportunity because I was intimidated by the concentration of power in the room.

I realize now that I needed to walk into that room feeling confident and prepared. Number 8 in Gifford Pinchot's *Intrapreneur's 10 Commandments* is advice that I now live by: "Come to work each day willing to be fired." That's the posture it takes to influence executives, to be bold enough, prepared enough, and focused enough to risk it all for the sake of the user experience.

The Lesson: Executives Want to Be Inspired, Too

Meeting with senior leadership is about translating vision into action. Executives live in a world of competing priorities, relentless financial pressures, and endless proposals. Playing it safe rarely moves executives. As Pinchot's commandment reminds us, you need to be willing to risk something, to speak truthfully, boldly, and with conviction. When you combine evidence with a clear ask and the confidence to stand behind it, you give your vision the best chance to move from presentation to transformation.

Call to Action: Be Prepared

Preview your presentation with your boss. Listen to their feedback and suggestions. It helps to have a supporter in the room.

Come armed with evidence. Collect customer testimonials, usability data, and financial impacts that tie your vision directly to business results. Passion without proof rarely wins support.

Make a clear ask. End every executive meeting by requesting a specific action or decision to move the initiative forward.

Frame it for your audience. Follow up with leaders individually and connect the vision to their priorities. Show how UX can help them hit the goals they are accountable for.

Be bold, not timid. Adopt the mindset of Pinchot's intrapreneurial commandment. Come willing to risk something. Speak with conviction, even if it feels uncomfortable.

When Cool Is More Important Than Simple
The Cool Solution That Wasn't Usable

A few years back, my boss handed me a new project. As
sometimes happens, he did not just assign the work, he also

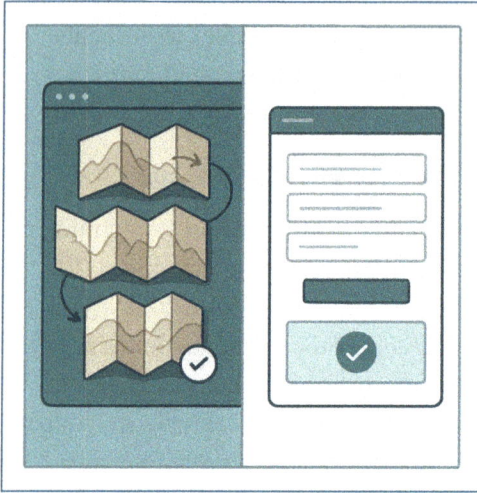

brought along the
"solution." He had
recently seen a flashy
application that used
unfolding animations,
like an old paper map
opening panel by
panel. Each section
revealed the next step
in the process, with
six panels in all,
culminating in
submitting the form.

To him, it was brilliant. To me, it was elevating "cool" at the
expense of usability.

I ran a quick analysis of the task itself. When you stripped away
the theatrics, the process boiled down to asking three simple
questions. There was no need for six steps or elaborate transitions.
Just ask the questions, submit the form, and let users move on with
their day.

I pulled together a short presentation comparing the simple
approach to the cool approach—six animated steps requiring six
answers and six navigation clicks—versus three straightforward
questions requiring three answers and one navigation click.

I explained that users of this small application were not interested
in a cool "experience." This was an app they were required to use
when returning from a trip and they wanted to get in and get out as
quickly as possible. What my boss saw as engaging, they would
see as unnecessarily complicated.

It was a classic UX dilemma: the tension between what looks exciting to stakeholders and what actually works for users. While visual design is important, sometimes the "cool" solution is the wrong solution. When an interface starts performing for performance's sake instead of expediting a tedious task, it stops being a tool and becomes a distraction.

The Lesson: Define Success Before You Measure It

When designing a mundane business app, I've often been asked to make it "cooler." When I ask them to define "cool," they can't tell me but they'll know it when they see it. Try designing that.

When evaluating alternative design solutions—especially with your boss—it's essential to first align on what "best" actually means. Is it the fewest steps? The least amount of time spent in the app? The simplest experience for the user? Contemporary visual design? Without a shared definition of success, even the most thorough analysis can lead to disagreement.

Call to Action: Define Success and Stick to It

Pause before building. When you are handed a "solution," resist the urge to dive straight into execution. Step back and ask: what is the real objective here?

Define success clearly. Before you design a solution, get agreement with stakeholders on what "better" actually means: fewer steps, less time, higher accuracy, or reduced frustration. Everyone should be judging designs by the same yardstick.

Validate competing designs. Use quick research, usability testing, or task analysis to ground the conversation in data, not opinion. If possible, have real users be the arbiter of alternatives.

Communicate with respect. Present your findings without dismissing other ideas outright. Show the contrast between "flashy but slow" and "simple but effective" in a way that clearly indicates which approach meets users' needs—but honor your sponsors and thank them for their input.

The UX Team (And You) Are Disrespected
A Presentation That Said More Than It Showed

I had been preparing to deliver a high-stakes presentation to the CIO, a rare chance for my UX team to be seen by a top executive.

Visibility at that level didn't come often, and I viewed it as a pivotal opportunity to demonstrate the strategic value of UX and the business impact our team was having.

I treated it like the career-defining moment it could have been. I wanted the story to be airtight, both for me and for my team, who deserved recognition at the executive level for their work.

I had two more weeks to prepare for the meeting when late on a Sunday night around 10 p.m., I logged in and saw an email that stopped me cold. Without explanation or notice, my calendar indicated that the presentation had been rescheduled to tomorrow morning!

I had been prioritizing my time based on having an additional two weeks to prepare my presentation. Now that time was gone, and I stayed up the entire night reworking slides and refining the narrative. The presentation itself went fine. But the silent schedule change made it clear how little my time, and by extension the work of the UX team, was valued.

That should have been my exit moment. But I stayed for my team. They were doing outstanding work, and I felt an obligation to shield them from the politics and dysfunction of the leadership team above me.

Unfortunately, things only deteriorated from there. Our group was placed under a leader with no understanding or interest in UX. Not long after, my entire talented team—including me—were laid off.

The Lesson: Respect is Not a Given

I've worked at companies where members of the executive leadership team were friendly, accessible, and appreciative of the contributions the UX team provided the company. I naively believed this would be true at all companies—until this total disregard for my needs and commitments occurred.

Assess the culture you're in. If leadership consistently disrespects, undermines, or devalues the work of your team, consider whether this an environment where UX can survive. If the answer is no, the most strategic move is to take your talent somewhere it will be valued and help your teammates do the same.

Call to Action: Try This First, but Start Your Job Search

Make yourself visible. Don't wait for leadership to stumble upon the value of UX. Make your own appointments with executives and be sure to include your direct manager. Make it impossible for them to overlook your contributions by regularly showing the impact of your work in ways that connect to their priorities. Tie your stories to outcomes executives care about.

Advocate for your team. Elevate their contributions in every interaction with leadership. Recognition boosts morale and demonstrates that UX is a team discipline.

Know when to walk away. Protecting your team sometimes means recognizing when your position is no longer tenable. If leadership continually disrespects you, and by extension, your team, the healthiest choice may be to start planning your exit.

Reaching a Tipping Point
When Culture Pushes Back

Sometimes, no matter how hard you try, you can't outrun a development-driven corporate culture.

At one company I worked for, a remarkably courageous UX advocate managed to pull off what I thought was impossible: convincing a multi-national, engineering-led organization to support a corporate-wide user experience team. And he did not do it by marching in, waving the UX banner, and demanding change. He was far more strategic than that.

He started by tasking the new team around building internal SGML tools to produce documentation. This was an easier sell in an engineering-heavy culture. But slowly he evolved the charter of the group into an internal UX consultancy offering best practices, user-centered methods, and hands-on support to product teams across the company. By the time corporate leadership realized the transformation was happening, the UX mindset had already taken root.

I joined in the middle of that transition. We framed design work in engineering terms, measured outcomes in terms of human-product system performance, and earned credibility by linking the human experience back to reduced costs and increased competitiveness. It was a delicate balance, but it worked.

For five years, the team delivered enormous value. We helped developers solve stubborn design problems and quietly seeded a user-first mindset in places it had never existed before. But despite all our progress, our founder was fighting uphill every day to justify the team's existence and prove its worth.

Eventually, the constant battles took their toll. The politics, the resistance, and the weariness of always needing to explain and defend us wore him down. Finally, he made the painful decision to walk away and dissolve the team.

It was the end of a bold experiment that had shown much promise, but ultimately could not be sustained in the current culture.

The Lesson: Cross-Functional Allies Are Critical for UX

Even the best UX teams struggle to survive when the surrounding culture is not ready or willing to change. One visionary leader can open doors and create momentum, but unless others pick up the banner, the effort risks collapsing the moment that leader steps away. Sustainable change requires a coalition: multiple voices across functions who can defend, reinforce, and normalize user-centered practices.

Call to Action: Measure Value and Publicize Your Efforts

Build a coalition. Do not rely on one champion. Recruit allies across product, engineering, marketing, and support. Make sure multiple voices are advocating for your UX initiatives, so the vision does not collapse if one leader leaves. (See Volume 1—People—of *Navigating the Politics of UX* for advice.)

Share the credit. Position UX outcomes as cross-functional wins. When others see that supporting UX increases their own corporate visibility, they are more likely to advocate for your team.

Document successes and collect testimonials. Report quarterly with revenue generated, costs that were saved, market penetration, and customer testimonials in quotes and videos.

Engage other voices. Enlist your allies to tell stories of how your UX team helped them be successful. Their voices will speak louder than yours.

When Business Fads Become Religions
Working in Corporate Cults

Every five to ten years, a new business philosophy sweeps through the corporate world. It arrives with bold promises of

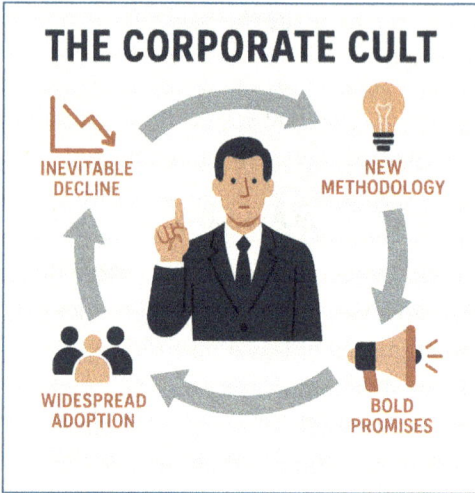

transformation, a slick acronym, and often a near-religious following. Over my career, I have watched one movement after another take its turn in the spotlight: Quality Function Deployment, Hoshin Planning, Lean, Six Sigma, Reengineering, Design Thinking, Agile, and many more.

Each fad arrives with great fanfare. Executives issue company directives. Consultants arrive as high priests. Certifications are created. Sacred rites are practiced.

When I worked at one company, the devotion to Six Sigma was so absolute that the lobby in every building proudly posted the sign: "Six Sigma—The Way We Work" as if Six Sigma was *the* business process to end *all* business processes, never to be supplanted. These movements always claim to put people at the center, but in practice, only a few are grounded in the lived experiences of employees or customers.

Most business movements are rooted in sound thinking and have a place, but not in every place. For example, Six Sigma practices made sense in manufacturing but most had no place in UX design. When organizations stop treating them as tools and start treating them as dogma, force-fitting them into disciplines where they don't belong, applying the framework itself becomes the ends rather than the means.

The tension is especially sharp in fields like UX. Our work is exploratory, nonlinear, and messy. Trying to funnel it into a process designed for manufacturing or finance creates activity without achievement. That said, we are still required to work within them. When I worked at that Six Sigma company, I co-created a two-day course that integrated Six Sigma language and metrics into the practices of human-centered design. It was awkward, but it worked, and it made HCD relevant in the corporate context.

The Lesson: Stay Grounded Through the Hype

Resisting the "method of the moment" rarely earns influence. The healthiest mindset is to treat every framework as exactly that: a tool. All have strengths worth borrowing, but none are universal solutions to human-centered design problems. Apply them where they fit, adapt them where they don't, and conduct yourself as a team player until the next one comes along.

Call to Action: Work Within Business Frameworks

Use frameworks as tools, not as rules. Treat every methodology as a resource in your toolbox, not as doctrine to be followed blindly.

Concentrate on outcomes over process. Guard against the trap of focusing on "doing the process right" at the expense of solving real user or business problems. Always measure progress against outcomes, not adherence to a checklist.

Stay flexible and wait it out. Even the most entrenched corporate fads eventually fade away. Adapt and remain compliant while the process is in vogue, but never let the process distract from your true mission. As long as you can still conduct research, cure customer pain points, and champion innovative solutions to customers' big unmet needs, you're doing your job.

Chapter 5: Leading Your UX Team

Throughout most of my career, I've found myself in some form of UX leadership role—sometimes as a manager or director, at other times as an individual contributor operating by influence rather than authority. You don't have to be a manager to be a leader in your company, but managers have an additional set of responsibilities that can be difficult to navigate.

I've always tried to lead others in the way I wanted to be led. I sometimes accepted management roles—not because I wanted to manage others—but because I didn't want to have the position filled by someone who didn't understand or value UX. My management philosophy was simple: hire great people, clear obstacles out of their way, and protect them from the chaos that too often trickles down from upper leadership.

In this chapter, I share some of the moments that have shaped my approach to leading UX teams. I've always believed that managing a creative team is a unique skill set, one that often conflicts with standard human resource department policies. Some of the practices I describe here may not fit easily within rigid corporate cultures, especially those built on control rather than trust. Nevertheless, I think you'll find many of the suggestions in this chapter to be helpful in leading your team, even when they violate some of your company's rules.

Design Jams
The Spark of In-Person Collaboration

There is something electric that happens when you gather a creative team around a tough problem, a whiteboard, a pile of Post-its®, and a shared sense of purpose. I have seen it countless times: the spark, the energy, the fast-moving flow of ideas that builds until someone exclaims, "Wait, what if we tried *this*?"

I have often argued that creativity does not thrive under fluorescent lights, rigid office hours, in sterile conference rooms, or featureless cubicles. But there is one exception: in-person design jams. Give a talented team a shared space, add markers, Legos®, maybe even a little music, and watch the magic unfold. People stop worrying about schedules and deliverables. They start feeding off one another's energy. Someone sketches a half-formed idea on the whiteboard, another extends it, and suddenly a third person makes the connection that unlocks the breakthrough.

This kind of generative collaboration does not translate to virtual sessions in Zoom or Teams. Virtual meetings have their place for updates, presentations, and some decision-making, but they can't replicate the energy of a live design jam. The lag in conversation, the lack of eye contact, and the flatness of the screen all drain the rhythm and tension that drive bold ideas.

While designers spend much of their time working heads-down in Agile cycles, there is no substitute for the moment when you put a team in the same room and turn them loose.

The Lesson: Collaborative Creativity Requires Presence

Innovation thrives when creative teams come together in the same room with a bold challenge. The energy, spontaneity, and collaborative breakthroughs that emerge in a live design jam do not translate in virtual settings. Distributed work has its place, but when the stakes are high and you are chasing bold ideas, it pays to invest in in-person collaboration.

Call to Action: Plan Your Next Design Jam

Plan for in-person design jams for big design challenges. Big, bold ideas require live energy. When kicking off a major initiative or when the team feels stuck, invest in bringing people together. Even once a quarter can make a difference.

Create the right environment for creativity. Choose a space that feels open and energizing. Stock it with whiteboards, sticky notes, markers, and prototyping tools. Add playful elements like Legos® or music to keep the atmosphere loose and generative.

Structure the sessions around short bursts. Work in focused blocks of two to three hours, then pause. Give your team downtime to reflect, sketch, and recharge. Often, the best ideas surface later, in the car, on a walk, or during a coffee break.

Capture and preserve the creative flow. If possible, dedicate a war room where sketches, notes, and half-baked concepts can live between sessions. Let ideas accumulate on the walls. Fresh eyes tomorrow may uncover insights today's session missed.

Include everyone in the momentum. If full-team travel is not feasible, gather co-located sub-teams for mini-jams, then reconvene virtually to stitch the pieces together. Find creative ways to connect ideas across locations.

Treat design jams as culture-building, not just problem-solving. The magic of these sessions is not only the solutions they generate but also the relationships they strengthen and the collaborative, creative culture they reinforce.

Field Trips
Getting Away to Recharge Team Batteries

As a UX leader, one of your most important responsibilities is creating opportunities for your team to learn and grow.

Conferences and training courses are valuable, but there is another form of learning that too few companies invest in: field trips.

I have always believed in the power of getting outside the building. Some of my most important insights came from walking through museums, visiting innovative companies, or spending time with experts in fields adjacent to UX.

One of my favorite practices was taking trips to the Smithsonian Institution to study how technology has evolved. Walking through the history of computing from room-sized mainframes to the first clunky personal computers, to the sleek smartphones of today was like watching UX evolution from complexity to simplicity in slow motion.

For my team, I arranged inexpensive visits to parks and coffee shops. Some were purely recreational and social, like boating and Top Golf trips. At the start of each new year, I hosted my team at my home for a planning meeting and fixed them lunch.

When we were embarking on adding gamification features to our products, we visited Carnegie Mellon to meet with the top game design scientist in the country. He asked us questions that reframed our entire approach. In one hour, he expanded our thinking more than weeks of whiteboard sessions ever could.

These simple excursions sparked conversations we would never have had inside an office.

The Lesson: Build Esprit de Corps with Field Trips

The most powerful insights often emerge when we step outside the building. Field trips, whether to museums, other companies, or even a local park, can spark the kind of thinking that no internal meeting ever will. They spark "*Aha!*" moments, shift perspectives, and sometimes unlock breakthrough ideas that transform products. As UX leaders, we should treat them not as extras but as essential tools for learning, bonding, and fueling innovation.

Call to Action: Plan Your Next Field Trip

Gather ideas from your team. At your next team meeting, ask for suggestions about where to go to get away from the grind and talk about new directions. Choose one and set it up.

Start local. You do not need a travel budget. Take your team to a nearby museum, library, store, or public space. Use the environment as a lens for exploring how people interact with tools, systems, or information.

Tie trips to real challenges. Frame field trips around problems the team is wrestling with. Seek out experts in the field and ask to meet with them.

Visit other companies. Reach out to peers from conferences or networks and arrange a visit. Seeing how other companies practice UX or prioritize customers can spark new approaches for your own team.

Capture and share insights. After each trip, debrief as a team. Document the takeaways and share them with leadership to make the value of field trips visible.

Managing Interpersonal Conflicts
When Roles Collide

The title "Product Owner" has always struck me as problematic. It can suggest, sometimes unintentionally, that the product belongs to

one person and that their decisions are final. In reality, while product managers or owners may be judged on market success, no single role should hold a monopoly on "owning" the product. Great products are always the result of collaboration.

At one company, several members of my UX team struggled with a particular product owner. She was deeply committed to her work, but she often made unilateral decisions that created friction with our designers. Most of the time, the team found ways to manage, but one pairing of a senior designer and this product owner reached a breaking point. Their conflicts threatened the project itself.

I tried to resolve the conflict by raising the issue with my boss, speaking with her manager, and trying to get the two assigned to different projects. This option was not possible; they had to find a way to work together.

The designer and the product owner eventually sat down and acknowledged the tension directly. Both admitted they did not enjoy working together. Rather than end the conversation there, they created a written working agreement outlining their roles, responsibilities, and shared values. Chief among these values was respect for each other's contributions, even when they disagreed.

As the UX director, I included the product owner in more UX activities, and ensured she was kept informed of all research visits and customer interactions. For a time, things settled down.

In the end, the personalities were too strong to get along, and my team member left the company. Sometimes, despite our best efforts, personality differences can't be managed away.

The Lesson: Sometimes Personal Clashes Can't Be Resolved

Written agreements can clarify responsibilities and values, giving people a neutral reference when conflicts arise. They also show a willingness to compromise.

But sometimes no amount of process or goodwill can overcome a lack of chemistry. Even then, efforts to acknowledge the tension and attempt a resolution can set a positive precedent for how to handle future conflicts.

Call to Action: Clarify Roles and Values

Get rid of the "product owner" title. Good luck with this. While this would have been the best solution, it probably won't happen.

Create working agreements. Encourage teams to draft written agreements clarifying roles, responsibilities, and shared values. When conflicts arise, reset and remind everyone that you share the common goal of designing a successful product, even when your ideas for achieving this goal may differ. Focus on what is right for the product rather than on being "right."

Be an advisor, not a referee. As a manager, when your teammate comes to you with a problem, your first instinct may be to intervene and resolve it. Don't use your power this way. Brainstorm solutions with them but rely on them to solve it.

Work with the other employee's manager to resolve the conflict. While neither of you should directly intervene (at least initially), you can share information to uncover the underlying reasons for the disagreements.

UX Strike Teams for Big, Urgent Problems
The Power of the UX Collective

UX designers are often handed a wicked-hard problem to solve and an impossibly short deadline. When that happens, I mobilize a

UX strike team: a swarm of the full team's diverse expertise, brought together to help one designer crack the problem in fresh, creative ways.

One of the most memorable times this happened was when we were given just two days to design a new application destined for the CEO. We set up in a war room, dissected the problem, traded questions and answers, pulled in subject-matter experts, and sketched ideas late into the night. We paused occasionally, allowing time for individual work, then reassembled to share our progress. By morning, we had a set of mockups ready.

When we showed the designs to the executive overseeing the project, he responded: *"This is freakin' awesome!"*

That's the magic of the strike team model. The lead designer always remains the face of the project. They own the problem and present the solution to the rest of the organization. But behind them is the collective power of the whole team: a chorus of perspectives, skills, and creative energy converging on one hard challenge.

The Lesson: UX Strike Teams Are Innovation Generators

High-pressure projects reveal the strength of a UX team's culture. When a single designer is asked to solve an impossibly hard problem on a tight deadline, isolating them almost guarantees burnout and missed opportunities. But when the whole team rallies, bringing different skills, perspectives, and creative instincts, the results can surpass what any one person could achieve alone.

The strike team model works because it channels urgency into collaboration. It's not about taking ownership away from the lead designer, but about surrounding them with a surge of support that multiplies their impact. This requires a culture of humility, and a shared understanding that the team's diversity of skills and perspectives is ultimately what makes the UX function successful.

Call to Action: Mobilize a UX Strike Team

Foster a culture of collaboration before the crisis hits. A strike team can't succeed if individuals are territorial or competing for credit. Build an environment where asking for help is encouraged and collaboration is the default behavior.

Maintain ownership of the design problem. The lead designer remains the face of the project and has ultimate decision authority.

Set the stage for intensity. When the team swarms on a problem, dedicate a physical or virtual "war room" where focus is uninterrupted.

Leverage diversity. Draw on the full range of skills in your team: research, visual design, prototyping, systems thinking, etc. Encourage everyone to bring their unique perspectives to the problem. Individuals may not be "unicorns," but collectively the UX team is.

Structure the swarm. Balance individual heads-down time with co-design sessions. Allow individuals to explore directions independently, then reconvene to refine and merge the strongest ideas.

Celebrate the wins. After the pressure cooker ends, reward the team's effort, highlight what was learned, and reinforce the pride of having delivered something extraordinary together.

Managing Employees in Trouble
Finding a Place for Misaligned Roles

I once had a direct report who was struggling in his role. Despite his best efforts, he couldn't keep up with the demands of the job.

Colleagues and leadership raised concerns, and he was placed on a formal performance improvement plan with three months to turn things around or be laid off.

Instead of treating the plan as a prelude to failure, I reassessed his situation. His skills did not match the high-concept strategy work the role demanded, but he had other strengths: he was highly organized, calm under pressure, and excellent at managing complex logistics without losing track of details.

Those qualities were not the ones we typically recruited on a UX team, yet they were exactly what we needed to make other members of our team more productive.

Rather than forcing him into a mold he did not fit, I created a new role that was more operational in nature, where he could focus on making the UX team run smoothly. He thrived in that role, brought order and clarity to our projects, and made all of us work more efficiently.

The Lesson: People Are Not Disposable

Not every performance problem is about capability; many are about alignment. When someone struggles in a role, it is easy to assume they are not a fit for the team or the organization. By looking beyond the narrow definition of a job description, we can uncover hidden strengths that can serve the team in different ways. A well-placed adjustment can transform a struggling employee into an essential contributor while strengthening the team as a whole.

Our responsibility as managers is not just to evaluate performance but to recognize potential. When we help someone find the right fit instead of writing them off, we create lasting value for both the business and for our employees.

Call to Action: Actively Manage Performance Improvement Plans

Diagnose the root cause of performance struggles. Before assuming a lack of ability, ask whether the problem stems from misalignment between the role's demands and the individual's strengths.

Identify hidden strengths. Look for what the individual does well, including organization, communication, or facilitation. These strengths often sit outside the role's job description.

Look for other ways the employee can contribute. Consider how those strengths could be redirected to serve the team or the organization differently. Determine whether responsibilities can be adjusted or a new role created.

Adjust the role when possible. Restructure tasks and responsibilities to better align with the person's skills. This strengthens both the individual and the team.

Craft the performance improvement plan. Design the plan to make the most of the employee's strengths. Document how the new responsibilities will contribute to the team and to the business. Measure results monthly.

Meet weekly with the endangered employee. Provide feedback, encouragement, and recognition of their progress. Match their activities and deliverables to the performance improvement plan and share measurable results with your boss.

Performance Evaluations
The Broken Math of Performance Reviews

Every year, when performance review season rolled around, I thought about quitting my job. I loved the work, the people, and the challenge of building innovative products. But the review process felt less like recognizing contributions and more like reducing people to numbers.

At one company, managers had to rate employees across fourteen core competencies on a scale of one to five, and then roll them into a master spreadsheet containing the ranking numbers for everyone in the division. It looked objective and fair, but in practice, the numbers were meaningless. One year, the top-ranked employee according to the spreadsheet was laid off a few months later.

In another company, we held calibration meetings. Managers gathered around a table, jockeying to fit their employees into the limited slots at the top. The quiet, invisible, and politically unconnected employees were always the easiest to move down. Meanwhile, the visible ones rarely lost their place in the upper echelon. Salary increases were based on performance bands.

After the rankings came the one-on-ones. The system required "balanced feedback," which meant inventing "weaknesses" or "improvement opportunities" where none existed. Recognition turned into demoralization.

I hated it, so I tried to play the game according to my own rules. I gave everyone the highest rating—not because they were flawless, but because the process was broken. When told I could not do that again, I rotated the top performers from year to year, ensuring if you didn't get a big raise this year, you would get one next year.

But the real reviews happened outside the spreadsheets. I took each person to lunch and asked: What new skills do you want to develop? Where do you want to be a year from now, and how can I help? Most importantly, I shared where the UX team needed to go in the coming year, how they could contribute, and conveyed how important they were to our team's success. I ended with: "You've done great work this year. But it's not your *best* work. Your *best* work is ahead of you." Of course it is. Who would want to believe otherwise?

The Lesson: Performance Celebrations

Performance reviews are supposed to recognize contributions and plan for future growth, but too often they become box-checking exercises that reduce people to numbers. Instead, reimagine the review as a coaching conversation. Both you, the manager, and the direct report should come out of the meeting feeling proud, inspired, and looking forward to the upcoming year.

Call to Action: Spend 10% on the Past, 90% on the Future

Redefine the review as a conversation, not a score. Take the employee to lunch and share your goals for the future. Ask the employee to share theirs and find common ground. Forget about your roles as boss and employee for an hour and just be colleagues with a common passion for UX.

Celebrate strengths, and don't manufacture weaknesses. Acknowledge what your team members did well and how it impacted the company, the product, or the customer.

Use the system, but don't be bound by it. Play the ratings game, but make sure your people know the real story is not the number in HR's spreadsheet. It is the value they bring to work every day.

Communicate how much the team needs them. Spend 10% of the meeting talking about the past and 90% talking about the future and how essential that person is for future success. Make it clear the team can't succeed without them.

Pick Your Battles Wisely
Don't Sweat the Small Stuff

Not every usability issue is worth your time and energy. You must pick your battles carefully.

CHOOSING BATTLES

Once my team was fired up about a particular readability violation. An End User License Agreement (EULA) in one of our applications was written in all caps. They immediately wanted to raise this as a usability infraction, and they were not wrong. All-caps text is harder to read.

The team was ready to march into a product review armed with academic studies and readability guidelines to make the case for converting the EULA into standard sentence-case formatting.

But we were supporting multiple products with dozens of usability issues that had a far greater impact on the customer experience.

So I asked a simple question: "Has anyone here actually *read* this EULA?"

After a pause, someone muttered, "Well... no."

I followed up: "When you install other software, do you read their EULAs?"

Another round of "Nos."

If no one was reading the EULA, then fighting for sentence case was not going to significantly affect the user experience. There was no experience. We needed to focus our energy on the issues that truly shaped the user's success like navigation flaws, workflow breakdowns, and confusing terminology.

The Lesson: All Usability Defects Are Not Created Equal

In a world of limited time and resources, if we waste energy on battles that do not meaningfully affect the user experience, we risk being seen as nitpicky, or worse, irrelevant. When that happens, we lose the credibility we need to tackle issues that really matter.

Call to Action: Address Critical Pain Points, Defer the Rest

Define the stakes. Before escalating a usability issue, ask: Will solving this problem help users accomplish their goals more quickly, more easily, or with less frustration? If the answer is no, it may not be worth worrying about.

Prioritize impact over principle. Keep a running list of usability concerns, but focus your advocacy on those with the greatest effect on user success, business outcomes, or both. Just because an issue is on your heuristic checklist doesn't mean you should correct it, at least not now.

Spend political capital wisely. Save your strongest arguments and your seat at the table for the issues that matter. Constantly arguing to address minor infractions can earn you a reputation as a zealot who is unwilling to compromise.

When Failure Fuels the Breakthrough
From Failure to Hero

I once had the privilege of leading a truly remarkable UX team. On every project, they exceeded expectations, delivering designs

that delighted users and impressed stakeholders. But one project reminded us that even the best teams can stumble.

We were tasked with designing a brand-new experience for a notoriously diverse audience, many of whom had short attention spans and limited experience with technology. The solution needed to be visually engaging and radically simple. After weeks of iteration, we presented our concepts to senior leadership.

The next day, the CTO pulled me aside. He was measured in his criticism, but made it clear that the leadership team was disappointed with our designs.

Hearing that kind of feedback is discouraging, especially when you know how hard your team has worked. I immediately called the team together and conveyed the feedback I had received. But I knew we couldn't afford to wallow in our failure; we needed to immediately move past this setback and take action.

I told the team: "This is your chance to be heroes! No one, not even our competitors, has solved this design problem for this audience. But I know you are the team to do it."

I gave them their marching orders and left them to decide how to proceed. Three days later they came back with not *one* new design, but *four*, each bold, distinct, and imaginative.

This time, when we shared the work with our stakeholders, the response was overwhelmingly positive. Confidence in the team was restored. What had begun as a crushing setback became one of our biggest wins.

The Lesson: Turning Setbacks into Momentum

Rosabeth Moss Kanter once said, "In the middle, everything looks like a failure." The path to success almost always runs through what, in the moment, appears to be a failure. What matters is how you respond when it shows up.

Failure is discouraging in UX, but it can also be liberating. Once the fear of achieving perfection is stripped away, teams are often emboldened to explore riskier and more innovative ideas.

Call to Action: Use Failure as a Springboard to Success

Reframe failure as a challenge. Meet with your team immediately when failure shows up. Share the feedback you received, then challenge them to come up with three new concepts to show to stakeholders. Give them a deadline; urgency can stimulate creativity.

Envision future success. Remind your team that this is their chance to solve a problem that has never been solved before. They are breaking new ground, so all constraints are off. Inspire them; redefine the temporary failure as a hero's quest.

Leave them alone. Let them get to work wherever they feel inspired. Set a time to check in at the end of the day to offer support and clear any hurdles.

Close the loop with leadership. When rebounding from a failed attempt, present new solutions with confidence. Emphasize how your team listened to their feedback and quickly responded to address their concerns. Trust in the team's ability to deliver great work will not just be restored, it will be stronger than ever.

Motivating Your Team
The Most Powerful Motivator is "Thank You"

For decades, business leaders have argued about the best way to motivate employees. Is it higher salaries? Bigger bonuses? Stock

options? Fancy perks? Recognition in meetings?

Those things are important, but in my experience, the most powerful motivator is not a bigger paycheck or a recognition from an executive. It's a genuine expression of thanks from a customer.

Seeing your work make a difference in a customer's life is the best reward of all. The morale boost—from an unsolicited note of appreciation from a customer, receiving a five-star review on social media, or seeing a customer excited by a feature you just built—supersedes any incentive a manager can offer.

Send every member of the UX team into the field to observe customers at least once per year. If budgets get tight, use remote tools such as Zoom or Teams. These interactions are more than just research; they are morale builders that offer a direct connection between the UX team and the people they are designing for.

I remember one instance in particular where I was standing at the back of a room full of customers who were experiencing one of our product's newest features for the first time. The UX designer was with me, and when the customers broke into spontaneous applause when the demo concluded, she turned to me and said: "This is why I do what I do!"

Employee exposure to customers is good business. A survey by the British Chambers of Commerce found that more than a third of employees cite customer satisfaction as their top motivator. When people know they are making a difference, they show up with more energy, more creativity, and more commitment.

The Lesson: Facilitate Customer Contact for Everyone

In the rush to meet deadlines with limited resources, it's easy to forget why we're building a product and who we're designing for. Reminding ourselves that we work for the customer—not just our bosses and our companies—is a simple notion but a remarkably powerful one. Without regular exposure, customers are just abstractions—generic "users" at worst or fictional personas at best. The connection between your teammates and the people who use the products they design needs to be direct and unfiltered.

Call to Action: Operationalize Customer Contact

Send your team into the field. Don't rely on secondhand reports and other people's customer stories to motivate your team. Seeing customers struggle firsthand is far more powerful than reading about pain points in a slide deck. And the emotional impact of hearing customers describe how a product has made their lives easier cannot be reproduced by any other means. Require at least one customer contact per year—many more if possible.

Make the voice of the customer an essential part of your UX practice. Besides customer visits, find other ways to expose employees to customers. Establish regular touchpoints such as customer councils, usability tests, listening in on support calls, attending training sessions, and accompanying account executives on sales visits.

The Demoralizing Effect of Outside Agencies
Insulting In-House "Junior Varsity" UX Teams

Over my years of leading in-house UX teams, one thing always made me angry: being told by my boss to bring in an outside

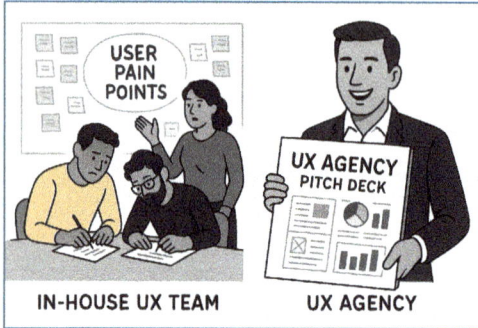

IN-HOUSE UX TEAM   UX AGENCY

agency to lead a major project. It was not framed as an opportunity to collaborate or a need to augment our capacity. The unspoken message was that our internal team was good enough for everyday work, but when the stakes were high, leadership wanted the "A-team."

I have seen this attitude at more than one company. A high-profile initiative would get the green light, and along with it, a large budget. Almost immediately, leadership would instruct me—the UX director—to hire a big-name consultancy. The agency would arrive with great energy, run workshops, interview stakeholders, and fill whiteboards. Within weeks, they would deliver a slick, beautifully packaged presentation with dozens of slides layered with strategy, personas, and polished visuals.

But their work was rarely implemented. It was not because they lacked talent. These agencies were filled with sharp, creative people. The problem was context. They didn't understand the intricacies of our business, the subtle but critical needs of our users, or the quirks of our culture and systems. Despite their polish, they could not bring the same depth of knowledge that my team had cultivated over years of mastering the product and the people who use it. In the end, it fell to the internal UX team to rework or completely redesign the agency's solutions so they would comply with the constraints of the real world.

In addition, the unspoken message to the internal team was that they are "junior varsity;" the *real* UX pros work in the outside agencies. Even as we quietly salvaged their work, we were left to wrestle with the reality that our own leaders did not trust us with the most mission-critical challenges. That lack of trust carried long-term consequences, undermining morale and making it harder to retain the very talent the company relied upon.

The Lesson: Trust Your Internal Talent

Hiring outside agencies to lead major initiatives may look like a quick win, but it often creates hidden costs in both execution and morale. Agencies can bring fresh perspectives, but they rarely have the depth of domain knowledge that internal teams have. Without that context, their solutions often require extensive rework.

When high-profile projects consistently bypass in-house teams, the implicit message is that internal talent is second-class. Over time, this demoralizes the very people who are best positioned to deliver sustainable innovation. Organizations that undervalue their internal UX teams are undermining their own future.

Call to Action: Elevate the Reputation of the Internal Team

Make your team's expertise visible. Provide quarterly updates highlighting the UX team's accomplishments. Publish a monthly newsletter with results from recent research, accolades from customers, and current initiatives. Invite other departments to write articles testifying to the successes delivered by partnering with the internal team.

Position your team as the bridge. When agencies are brought in, frame your team as the essential link between bold ideas and pragmatic delivery. Instead of competing, show how you can ground the agency's vision in business realities. Make it clear that outside agencies work for, and are supervised by, the internal UX team. Always co-present progress reports to leadership.

Create your own pitch for major projects. If told to seek outside consultants, before complying create your own pitch illustrating the benefits of keeping the project in house.

Managing Time
You Can't Schedule Inspiration

It is 2 p.m. on a Wednesday. The morning was productive, but now your energy has waned. You have been wrestling with a complex design problem for hours, staring at the same pixels, hoping for a spark of brilliance that refuses to come. And yet, because the end of the workday is still hours away, there you sit, in a 10x10 cubicle, eyes on the screen, the green presence dot glowing. Because that's what is expected of you: sit at your desk for eight hours a day, whether the ideas come or not.

But creativity doesn't work that way.

I remember trying the "Crazy 8s" exercise from Jake Knapp's book, *Sprint*. Sketch eight solutions in eight minutes. At first, I didn't think I could do it, but the timebox forced me to concentrate. By minute eight, I had generated several directions I never would have thought of at a slower and more deliberate pace.

But imagine doing the equivalent of Crazy 8s for eight hours a day, five days a week. That's 2,400 "ideas" every week. But idea generation is not the hard part. The real work is evaluating, discarding, prioritizing, refining, testing, and iterating those ideas until the best concept emerges.

Designers, often a company's most valuable source of innovation, burn out quickly when forced to produce brilliance on demand. Creativity needs the subconscious to churn in the background while the conscious mind takes a walk, reads a book, or plays with a child. You can tighten bolts on an assembly line for eight hours straight, but you can't manufacture great ideas that way.

When I led internal design teams, I told them that one lightning-strike idea born from thirty minutes of inspiration is worth more than forty hours of drizzle sitting at your desk. If that spark is not coming, step away.

The Lesson: Creativity Can't Be Clocked

Managers often track the time employees sit at their desks but don't give credit for the hours away from the office when they are thinking about work. Time away from the desk is not time away from working on a problem. For creative professionals, the freedom to step away is a necessity for doing exceptional work.

Breakthroughs often emerge at unexpected times when you have the right mindset to process complexity, form new connections, and arrive at insights that linear thinking alone can't achieve.

Call to Action: Measure Results, Not Time

Redefine productivity. Stop equating hours at a desk with hours spent working. Instead, measure outcomes like insights uncovered, problems solved, and breakthroughs delivered.

Give your team permission to step away. Normalize walking, reading, or unplugging as part of the design process. Creativity thrives when the mind has room to wander.

Protect time for reflection. Build buffers into project timelines so designers can digest complexity, test ideas, and let solutions emerge organically.

Foster trust over control. Replace green-dot monitoring with a culture of autonomy with accountability. Trust your team to manage their own creative process in ways that produce results.

Places that Inspire
Inspired Ideas Require Inspiring Settings

Several years ago, I was traveling across the country delivering workshops on my approach to user experience research, analysis, and design. I had developed a process and a series of carefully crafted questions that consistently led participants to uncover multi-million-dollar solutions to their toughest design challenges. And time after time, it worked.

Every city meant another sterile hotel conference room with beige carpeting, flickering fluorescent lights, and blank white walls. The rooms were functional but fell far short of the inspirational setting I wanted to provide for myself and my participants.

By the time I reached Seattle, the workshops had become routine. The energy that infused my earlier sessions had disappeared, and I found myself rushing through the material without allowing sufficient time to pause, reflect, and let it sink in.

About an hour into the session, I stopped midslide and led the group outside to the hotel lawn where we were under open sky, surrounded by trees, breathing fresh air, and hearing birds instead of HVAC fans. I left the slides behind; I didn't need them. What I needed was renewed inspiration and an environment where I could engage with the group in meaningful conversation.

Freed from the sterile walls, people began to share their stories. They collaborated and encouraged each other and solved problems that mattered. The energy was just what I—and they—needed.

The Lesson: Space Shapes Thinking

Innovation does not happen on command in a fluorescent-lit box. Sometimes, the best way to unlock creativity is to simply open the door and step outside.

As leaders, our job is not to police where people work. It's to create conditions for creativity where they can do their *best* work. That may mean holding meetings outdoors, in an art museum, or in a space that reflects the scale of the challenges we are tackling.

Giving teams permission to work in spaces that energize them is not an indulgence; it's an investment in the company's future. If you want breakthrough thinking, then break through the idea that all work must occur in cubicles and conference rooms.

Call to Action: Think Outside the Cubicle

Create an Ideas Room. Find an unused space in your company and designate it as a place where employees can imagine and create. Fill it with comfortable furniture, whiteboards, flip charts, toys, and other artifacts to encourage innovative thinking.

Take your team meetings outside. Even a short session in a courtyard, park, or rooftop can break the monotony and spark fresh ideas.

Curate inspirational spaces. Consider venues such as parks, art galleries, museums, or libraries that naturally provoke imagination and reflection.

Let your teammates work where they need to work. For big design challenges and tight deadlines, let your teammates check out from the office for a few days and work where they can be most productive. It could be at home on their back porch, in a cabin in the mountains, or sitting by a stream in a state park.

Embed location flexibility in your UX micro-culture. Normalize stepping away from desks for important creative work. If you work in a controlling culture, cover for your employees when the boss comes around wondering why someone is not at their desk.

The UX-Support-Content Partnership
Merging All UX Skillsets into One Team

In the most successful team I ever led, we had all the essential customer-facing disciplines in one department: content strategy,

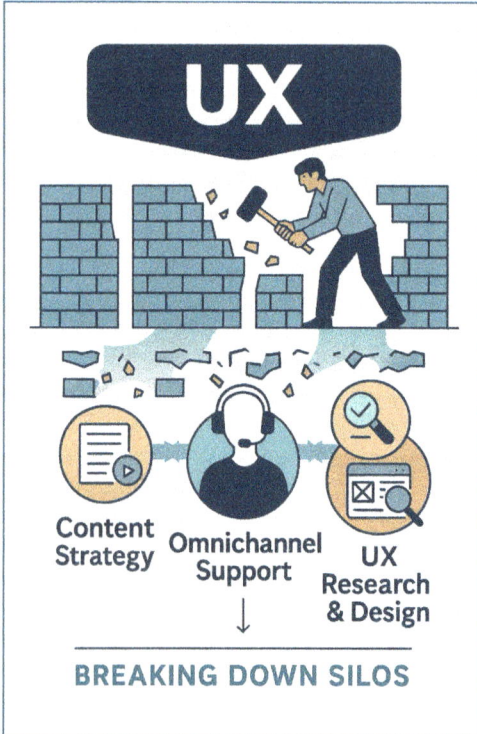

omnichannel support, and user research and design. It made perfect sense. After all, what is "the user experience" if not the seamless weaving together of all these elements?

Our content strategists understood that information was not just something you dumped into a manual. They worked hand in hand with product designers to ensure interface text was clear, concise, and devoid of jargon. They wrote user manuals and installation guides, yes, but they also reimagined what support documentation could be, authoring it in plain, approachable language that made even the most complex systems appear simple.

We also took on omnichannel support, something that had always been hidden away in websites and knowledge bases designed for internal agents rather than for end-users. Instead of sending people off to hunt through external resources, we embedded critical support information directly into the product. Walkthroughs, instructions, and videos were delivered at the exact moment and place the customer needed them.

And of course, we had UX designers and researchers who brought the skills of deep observation, workflow analysis, data visualization, and graphic design to transform insights into elegant, intuitive experiences.

What made it work was the respect the roles had for each other. There were no turf wars and no silos, just a collegial culture and a shared commitment to making our customers' lives easier. Together, we delivered experiences that felt seamless because, behind the curtain, our organizational structure truly was seamless.

The Lesson: Breaking Down Silos Creates Breakthroughs

The user experience is never the product of a single discipline. It is the sum of every touchpoint, every message, and every moment of interaction a customer has with your product. When those disciplines operate in silos, the seams show, and users feel the gaps.

Call to Action: Create the Org Chart Around the User

Map the touchpoints. Start by identifying every way your customers interact with your product. Analyze whether these areas are organizationally aligned or still live in silos.

Bring disciplines together. If content strategy, support, and UX research and design live in separate organizations, create cross-functional working groups and joint initiatives. Don't wait for a reorganization to start breaking down the walls.

Embed support and documentation into the product. Stop treating knowledge bases, FAQs, and user guides as separate from the user interface. Instead, put help where and when the user needs it, inside the experience itself.

Champion the shared mission. Frame your UX org not as "product design" but as the team responsible for end-to-end customer success. That small shift in identity makes collaboration among the functions necessary and natural.

Co-Design and Co-Coding with Developers
No More Throwing Designs Over the Wall

Development and UX can sometimes feel like rival camps, each perceived as making more work for the other. In one of my jobs, the development manager came close to banning one designer from setting foot in the development department because his attitude was so demeaning and caustic when his pixel-perfect mockups were not followed exactly.

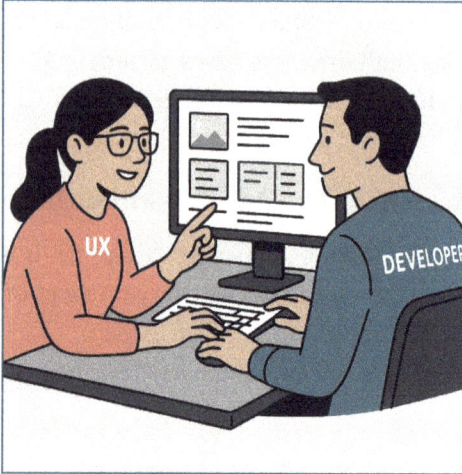

But it doesn't have to be this way. In another job, designers and developers were genuine collaborators, even friends.

As a UX manager, there's nothing more rewarding than seeing a designer and a developer sitting side by side at the same workstation, co-designing and co-coding a product. When a UX designer pulls up a chair alongside a developer to clarify desired interactions and help fine-tune the CSS, the designer-developer dynamic changes completely.

The best collaborations don't wait until the designer is ready to hand off high-fidelity mockups to development. The best result comes when designers share their work in progress and invite developers into the creative process early and often. This approach establishes a camaraderie between design and development, breaks down silos, and creates a sense of pride in shared ownership. It affords developers the opportunity to offer their own design ideas, and affords designers the opportunity to explain the rationale behind their design decisions.

When UX and development stop treating each other as separate functions and start working as co-creators, the result is a much better product than neither one could have produced alone.

The Lesson: Design and Development Are One Activity

In the old days, UX and development sat on opposite sides of a wall, both in reality and figuratively. Designers produced a pixel-perfect mockup, then would "throw it over the wall" for development to build, oblivious to the developer's time and technical constraints.

But when designers and developers sit shoulder to shoulder in partnership, the wall disappears. Solutions that neither partner would have thought of on their own are discovered. Questions are clarified in real time. Compromises are agreed upon. The results: better products that conform to schedule and technical constraints, *and* better working relationships between UX and development.

Call to Action: Co-Design and Co-Develop Your Products

Tear down the wall. Involve developers early in the design process and treat them as co-creators, not mere implementers.

Encourage shared ownership. Sit together, code together, and make decisions in real time.

Value works in progress. Share sketches, drafts, and prototypes before they are polished. Early visibility to the work in progress ensures the design direction is on course before it reaches development.

Respect technical constraints, but challenge them. Sometimes a developer's "no" is an opportunity for creative problem-solving. Real-time experiments can either prove a design is not technically feasible or generate new approaches that make it possible.

Leadership in the Face of Layoffs
Losing Members of Your Team

If you work long enough in this field, you will almost certainly experience a layoff. I have gone through four of them, sometimes personally and sometimes just for my teammates, each for different reasons. They are not a reflection of your worth or the quality of your work. They are numbers on a spreadsheet that drive decisions made far above your pay grade.

Once, I had the privilege of working for a company that handled an economic slowdown with an insightful and humane business strategy. Instead of cutting jobs, everyone worked nine out of ten days, with the tenth day unpaid, reducing salaries by ten percent. The philosophy was this: our employees are valuable, we have invested in their training, and we will need them again when the business rebounds. It engendered a loyal workforce that stayed in place long after the downturn ended.

Today, layoffs are usually the result of poor planning or short-sighted leadership. That's why I kept my UX teams lean so that we wouldn't be targeted for having more staff than leadership thought we needed. I am thankful that I never had to make the impossible choice of who stayed and who left. Those decisions always came from above.

When layoffs hit, my job was to lead the remaining team through the fear and pain of losing their colleagues. I immediately called a meeting, acknowledged what had happened, honored the people who had left, and helped the remaining team grieve, regroup, and move forward together. Leadership is all about honesty when layoffs happen, expressing empathy when morale is low, and showing strength when the uncertainty feels overwhelming.

In moments like these, your team is watching. What they need most is not a manager but a friend who sees them, stands with them, and expresses confidence that better days are ahead.

The Lesson: Layoffs Are an Unfortunate Norm

When layoffs occur, leadership's focus shifts from managing projects to caring for people. The survivors are consumed with grief, uncertainty, and sometimes guilt. You can't move on until you respect these feelings. A strong leader acknowledges the loss, honors those who have left, and helps the team find its footing again.

Layoffs test your leadership at its core. Teams do not remember polished talking points or business rationalizations. They remember whether their leader stood with them through this difficult time with expressions of genuine empathy and grief.

Call to Action: Lead Your Team Through the Trauma

Call the team together. Allow everyone to express their grief. Explain that layoffs are an unfortunate part of business life. Help them see the downsizing as a system failure, not a personal failure. However, saying "It's just business" is a terrible way to minimize the personal impact.

Tell your own story. If you have gone through layoffs before, tell them how things worked out for you. In my experience, once you get through the pain of rejection, you will often land a job that is better than the one you left.

Prepare for layoffs ahead of time. Sometimes people are shown the door before you get to say goodbye. Make sure you have personal email addresses for every member of your team in advance. Reach out and let them know you stand ready to provide them with references during their upcoming job search.

Chapter 6: Managing Your Career

Every few years, the UX profession finds itself at a crossroads. When I started, the challenge was simply convincing organizations that user experience mattered at all. Later, we had to prove that it could drive business results. Today, we face a new and more complex question: what happens when machines begin to design alongside us?

As of this writing, the UX job market is in the midst of one of the most uncertain phases I have seen in the past forty years. AI tools haven't eliminated UX roles outright, but professionals across the industry are trying to determine whether AI will become an indispensable ally or an existential threat.

What's undeniable is that UX practices are changing faster and more profoundly than at any time since our field began. This chapter proposes strategies for taking advantage of the AI revolution, but it also offers ideas on collaborating with your colleagues, interviewing for a new job, increasing your visibility, overcoming burnout, and developing the soft skills required to earn your place in the next generation of UX thought leaders.

Increasing Your Company-Wide Visibility
Finding, Owning, and Solving Problems

In the larger companies where I worked, cross-functional visibility was essential. Performance reviews and raises were not only about

doing your job well but also about standing out among equally qualified colleagues from development, marketing, support, and product management. Officially, everyone was evaluated on merit. Unofficially, only a fraction could

land in the top tier, and the majority were relegated to the middle. Five percent had to populate the lowest band.

To reach the top tier, your boss had to do more than advocate for you. Other managers needed to know who you were, remember working with you, and agree that you were a top performer. You had to be visible across the organization.

One of my early managers gave me advice I never forgot: "If you want to be visible, look for problems. When you find one, own it, even if it's not your job. Take responsibility for leading the solution."

UX has a unique advantage in this area. We can create interactive prototypes of our proposed solutions while most others can only describe theirs with bullet points on a PowerPoint slide. We combine deep domain knowledge with an understanding of customers, which allows us to notice problems others miss and visualize solutions in compelling ways.

Throughout my career, when I spotted a major unmet customer need, I prototyped potential solutions and enlisted other functions to help refine them. Doing so increased my visibility with executives, strengthened my reputation for leadership, and eventually gave me the freedom to choose my own projects rather than wait for my boss to assign them.

The Lesson: UX Sees Problems No One Else Can See

In large organizations, career growth often depends on being visible beyond your immediate team. For UX professionals, this means proactively identifying problems, even outside of your official responsibilities, and leading the charge toward solutions. Rapid prototyping, domain knowledge, and empathy for users give UX a unique edge: we can show possibilities while others can only talk about them. By seizing opportunities instead of waiting for assignments, you create both value for customers and the business while also shaping your career path.

Call to Action: Own the Problems You See

Watch for problems across multiple channels. Monitor call center logs, UX research, sales feedback, online reviews, and support records to identify recurring issues.

Select a high-stakes problem. Focus on a challenge that costs the company money, customers, or competitive advantage. Identify allies and sponsors who have a vested interest in solving it.

Prototype a solution. Create a quick, interactive prototype that addresses the pain point. The goal is not perfection but sparking conversation and showing that a better experience is possible.

Build support one-on-one. Meet individually with potential partners, especially those most affected. Show them the current experience, then walk them through your prototype. Invite them to refine the solution with you.

Assemble a cross-functional team. Bring together design, development, support, and sales. Assign responsibilities, create an action plan, and track measurable results.

Solving the Root Problem
The PIG and the Turning Point

Back in 1985, I was a technical writer at the computer workstation division of a multinational corporation. I had personally

experienced how difficult it was to connect and configure peripheral devices to our computers, and I proposed writing a manual that would be the single source of truth for assembling a working system. We had six computer models, three different operating systems, dozens of peripherals, fifteen types of interface cards, and a dizzying assortment of cables. Even our internal experts struggled to keep it all straight.

I wrote a massive, 500-plus-page manual called the Peripheral Installation Guide, fondly known as The PIG. It was comprehensive, accurate, well-written—and ultimately useless. When I visited customers, I couldn't help but notice their shelf of documentation with The PIG sitting there, still shrink wrapped and unread.

The PIG documented the complexity of our products but did nothing to reduce it. So, I reimagined the PIG as the "Intelligent PIG," a knowledge-based, interactive, software tool that guided users step by step through the installation procedure for their particular combination of computer, operating system, and peripherals.

I didn't call my approach "UX design" at the time, but that is what it was. I was starting to understand that my job was not to just document the system, but to simplify the experience of using it.

The Lesson: Solve the Root Problem

Documenting lengthy procedures does not solve the problem of complexity. It abdicates responsibility, in effect saying, "Simplifying the problem is too hard for us to solve, so just document it and let the user do it."

UX professionals don't think this way. But many of our colleagues do. I once talked to a support manager who pushed back on my attempts to simplify a product saying, "We don't want to make our products *too* easy to use—we make a lot of money on support contracts."

While others may be complacent, we must have the courage to speak up when something is broken. We may be the only people with the insight to reframe the problem in human, technical, and business terms, and have the tenacity to keep pushing for solutions that respect customers' time, attention, and priorities.

Call to Action: Advocate for Solutions Over Workarounds

Don't just point to problems, show the solution. Passionately advocating to solve complexity problems doesn't work. Show the solution with a prototype and compare the before and after states. Finally, wrap the solution in financial arguments: increasing market share and revenue, or reducing support and warranty costs.

Documentation and training expose complexity. Review your product's online help systems and product support articles. If you find lengthy step-by-step procedures, lots of technical terminology, demands to find and supply information, and lengthy explanations of foreign concepts, you just discovered a minefield of complexity. Don't wait for your next assignment. Solve the problem! But do so diplomatically, positioning your ideas in ways that empower those with the authority to act.

Expanding Your Job Description (And Your Impact!)
Turning Documentation into Designs

Early in my career, I led a small and remarkably talented team of technical writers. Like many writing teams of the time, we were

measured by our ability to produce clear, comprehensive documentation.

But we didn't just write. We also conducted research. We attended customer visits and usability tested our manuals to determine whether our instructions were easy to find and follow.

Through our research, we discovered that one of the product's most sophisticated features—requiring over 100 pages of instructions—was almost never used. The feature had the potential to save customers time and improve their outcomes, but it was simply too hard to understand and operate.

When I raised the issue with our development partners and leadership, I commiserated with them. I told them it was too bad that the expertise and investment that had gone into building the feature was largely unnoticed by customers. The company had created something powerful, but its value was hidden behind complexity and documenting it was not solving the problem.

One member of my team had strong technical skills, so we built a prototype of a lightweight application that acted as an intelligent front end to the product. It simplified the feature into a few guided steps.

Unfortunately, the prototype never went into production. A reorganization shifted priorities, and the project was shelved. Yet the experience convinced me that the best way to solve for complexity is not to *document* it, but rather to *design* it out of the user experience. This started my transition from technical writing to UX design.

The Lesson: Documentation Reveals Design Gaps

Documentation can uncover systemic usability problems by highlighting where complexity has crept into the user experience. But insight alone is not enough. Turning those insights into impact requires political acumen, strategic framing, and cross-functional alliances. Even the best solutions can stall if attention is not paid to the political undercurrents in the organization.

The most powerful contributions often come when you step outside your defined role, connect content strategy with UX strategy, and work with allies to design away the need for complex documentation.

Call to Action: Think Beyond Your Role

Expand content strategy to include design. Don't stop at documenting complexity. When the tools in your job description fall short, explore new approaches that elevate your contribution and remove UX pain points.

Prototype bold alternatives. Learn at least one prototyping tool well enough to show your ideas clearly. If you lack technical skills, partner with someone in development who can bring your concepts to life.

Build alliances with developers. Identify sympathetic partners who see the value in your non-documentation solution and provide technical credibility. Share credit with them when you pitch your ideas to leadership.

Show the potential of the solution, but don't finish it. Avoid polishing the prototype until it's perfect. Create a strong starting point and invite others to shape it. Collaboration turns potential resistance into shared ownership.

Getting Hired Through a Screen
The Limits of Virtual Interviews

Ever since the pandemic, remote interviewing has become the default for many companies. Instead of flying candidates in and

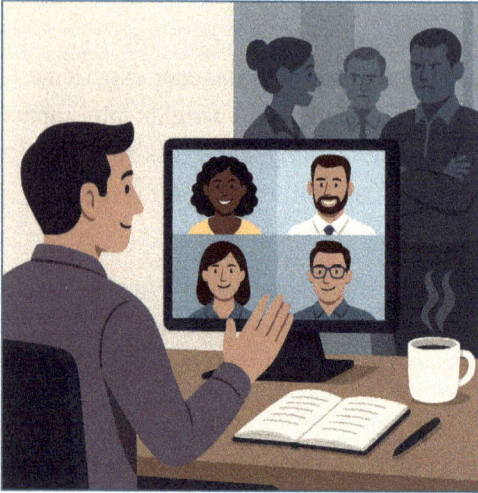

meeting them face to face, hiring managers rely on Zoom or Microsoft Teams for virtual interviews. It saves money and seems efficient for both the business and the candidates.

But efficiency has its limits.

Long before the pandemic, I went through a fully virtual interview myself. The hiring manager was about to go on leave, so to speed things up she interviewed me by phone and video conference. Based on the strength of my résumé and a couple of virtual conversations, she hired me. I didn't meet her in person for another three months.

The job turned out to be a poor fit for both of us.

The company culture clashed with my philosophy of UX. They had embraced the latest management fad and were trying to force-fit it into every aspect of their operations, including design. The process involved lots of activity, endless procedures, but very little real achievement. I wanted to innovate the UX practice; the company was more interested in compliance. My frustration started to show, and before long I knew I needed to leave.

A hiring decision is about culture fit as much as it is about skills and experience. Does the organization value what you value? Does it offer an environment where you can elevate the existing UX practice? The answers to these culture questions are difficult to assess through a couple of hours of remote interviews on a screen.

The Lesson: Probe for Culture Fit

Virtual interviews are here to stay. They are efficient and cost-effective. But culture fit is much harder to evaluate through a webcam. You don't see hallway conversations, overhear how teams talk to each other, or pick up on the subtle cues that reveal what life at a company is really like.

Recently, remote interviews have become even more problematic. I've talked to colleagues who have been interviewed by AI bots—as if "talking" to an artificial being offers any indication of the culture of your prospective work environment.

That's why you need to do more than simply answer questions and hope for the best. The responsibility falls on you to actively gather the information you need about the people, the culture, and the job expectations before you accept the offer.

Call to Action: Ask the Right Questions

Prepare your own questions. Do not wait for the "Do you have any questions for us?" at the end. Ask about culture, leadership style, UX maturity, attitudes toward innovation, approach to collaboration, and how decisions get made.

Assess the people, not just the process. Pay close attention to how your future manager and colleagues interact with you during the interview. Do they seem open, respectful, and curious, or rushed and dismissive? And personally, if I were interviewed by an AI bot, I would reject the job immediately.

Leverage outside sources. Use tools like Glassdoor reviews, LinkedIn connections, and informal chats with current or former employees to fill in the gaps that remote interviews leave behind.

Trust your instincts. If something feels off during a remote interview, don't ignore it. Your instincts are usually right.

Good Job Interviews and Bad Job Interviews
When the Right Job Comes Along, You'll Know It

Have you ever walked into a job interview and, within minutes, felt like you were talking to someone who truly groks you and

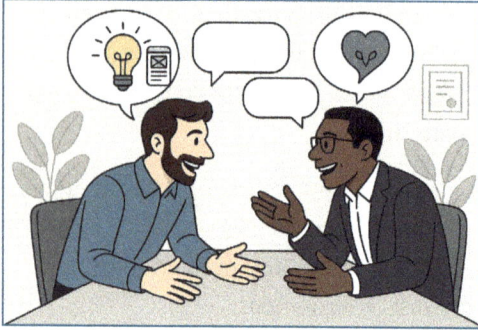

what UX is about? Not the kind of interview where you recite bullet points from your résumé or field stiff questions, but one where the conversation flows naturally. You swap ideas, finish each other's thoughts, and both feel energized by the discussion. In that moment, it's not about selling yourself. You walk out of the room not just *hoping* you will get the job but *knowing* you will.

I was fortunate to experience this in my first job. The manager who interviewed me was not just interested in checking skills off a list. He was kind, deeply passionate about his work, and genuinely curious about me as a person. That connection set the tone for what became an excellent working relationship.

It happened more than once in my career. Each time, those interviews felt less like interrogations and more like conversations between people who shared a common passion for the work. Sometimes the hiring manager would even pause mid-interview, smile, and say, "You're doing great." Those moments told me I was in the right place, surrounded by leaders who valued people over process.

I've also had the opposite experience. Interviews where the questions felt stiff and my answers were forced and awkward. It was clear the process was about filling a role, not building a team or advancing a vision. In one of those moments, a manager asked me the classic question: "So why do you want to work for our company?" Without thinking, I answered honestly, "I'm not sure that I do." Needless to say, I didn't get the job. And that was fine. If there is no real connection between the parties in the interview, it's not the right place to invest the next chapter of your career.

The Lesson: You'll Know When You Find the Right Fit

Let your passion for the work come through in interviews and look for the same on the other side of the table (or screen). Share what excites you about UX: the hard problems that you can't stop thinking about and the breakthroughs you've experienced that give you energy. When the conversation becomes a genuine exchange of ideas, you stop being just a candidate and start being a colleague in the shared quest to design the ideal experience.

This approach will not work with every interviewer. Pay attention to what the interviewer values and how your strengths align with their goals. Some hiring managers want a thought partner. Others are focused only on execution. Adjust accordingly.

Call to Action: Trust Your Instincts

Tell your stories. Share stories of how you influenced strategy, solved tough design problems, or turned research into impact.

Let your passion show. Talk about the challenges that drive you and the breakthroughs that inspire you. Enthusiasm is contagious and helps interviewers see you as more than a résumé.

Read the room like a researcher. Pay attention to cues. If the interviewer reflects your passion, dive deeper. If they focus on execution, highlight practical results. Tailor your responses as you would when interviewing customers.

Frame the conversation as collaboration. Show how you will work *with* them, not just *for* them. Position yourself as a strategic partner in advancing the organization's goals and helping your future boss succeed.

Close with confidence. Reinforce how your skills and approach to UX align with their vision. Leave them with a clear sense of how you will bring fresh perspectives to their organization.

Your Personal Need for Inspiration
Inspiration as Fuel for Job Fulfillment

Think about the last time you inspired someone. Maybe it was a colleague, a mentee, or an audience at a presentation. How did it feel to see their perspective shift, their energy lift, or their confidence grow?

Inspiration is fuel. When burnout creeps in, when the politics feel endless, when the spark seems gone, it is often the only thing that can cut through the fog. When you inspire someone else, you also inspire yourself.

If I can reach just one person with an idea that lands in a way that changes how they think or work, that is enough to help me overcome any disappointments I may face from day to day.

I will never forget a moment early in my career when I had the opportunity to present at a conference. The audience was not large, and I was still finding my footing as a speaker. But my topic was unique and offered an unusual twist on conventional wisdom. Afterward, a man came up to the podium, shook my hand, and said, "You changed my life."

Decades later, I still carry that moment with me. I don't know what I said that impacted him so deeply, but it inspired me to continue pursuing new ways of thinking about, and practicing, UX design. It has become a memory I return to, especially when I have been in roles that did not align with my passion, or when the uphill battles felt endless. It reminds me of why I do this work—not for recognition, but for the chance to rekindle the passion in someone else.

The Lesson: Inspire Yourself by Inspiring Others

Inspiration is a renewable resource, but only if you allow yourself to receive it as much as you give it. In the midst of deadlines, corporate politics, and the grind of daily work, it is easy for inspiration to run dry. The surest way to refill your own tank is by creating moments of inspiration for others.

Sometimes it comes through teaching, mentoring, or presenting at a conference. Other times it's as simple as sharing an idea or asking a question that unlocks new possibilities for a colleague. When you see that shift in someone's perspective, it can give you the energy to keep doing what you do.

Call to Action: Ignite and Share Inspiration

Instead of giving advice, ask questions. When a colleague comes to you for counsel, rather than giving advice, ask a question. Questions help people think about possible solutions they haven't thought about before. You can see it in their face when a question inspires them to go back to their desks and think about the problem in a different way.

Talk about ideas in your 1:1 meetings. Instead of just talking about the week's accomplishments and plans for the next week, share what you're thinking about. If something happened that revealed an unsolved design problem or a previously undiscovered customer need, share it and ask them to think about it, too.

Encourage your teammates to present at conferences. If you manage a UX team, encourage your direct reports to submit proposals to speak at industry conferences. They probably haven't considered their experiences to be worthy of sharing with others, but they're wrong. It's your job to develop the next generation of UX thought leaders.

Resolving Disagreements Over Key Decisions
You Win Some, You Lose Some

At some point in your career, you will find yourself at odds with colleagues over a decision that carries real weight for the team, the

product, or even the company. For me, one of those moments came when we were evaluating enterprise tools. The platform we chose would shape the way our UX and content design teams worked for years to come.

I had a clear favorite. I had done the analysis, tested the workflows, and believed strongly in my recommendation. But I was not alone. Others were equally convinced that a different tool was the better choice.

We each made our cases to leadership, laying out pros, cons, and long-term implications. When the decision was announced, my recommendation was not the one selected.

I was personally invested in the decision and felt defeated for days. But once the choice was made, I had to decide whether to keep fighting or to shift gears and make the most of the tool that had been chosen. I chose the latter.

Business is not about winning every debate. Sometimes the right answer is not obvious. Often the decision is not good versus bad, but good versus good. The real test is whether the selected solution addresses the problem at hand.

If it does, and your preference is not selected, let it go. It may feel that way, but a rejected recommendation is not a rejection of you. It's simply the way business operates. Keeping your focus on the bigger picture reinforces your reputation as a team player and earns you credibility for the next challenge.

The Lesson: Make Your Case, Then Support the Decision

When you find yourself on the losing side of a decision, pause before pushing back. Ask whether the chosen direction still solves the problem. If the answer is yes, shift your focus to making it successful.

Not every decision will go your way. Your professional effectiveness is not just measured by how many debates you win, but also by how you respond when the choice is not yours. Supporting the chosen path demonstrates your objectivity and professionalism. These traits accrue credibility over time, often more than a single victory ever could.

Call to Action: Practice Strategic Acceptance

Separate ego from outcome. A rejected recommendation is not a judgment of your worth. It is simply a business decision.

Support the chosen path. Once a direction is set, commit to making it successful. Colleagues and leaders will notice your response.

Keep perspective. Most decisions are not black and white. Focus on whether the solution addresses the core problem rather than on whose idea it was.

Play the long game. Show maturity and resilience when the decision goes against you. This sets you up for success in future debates.

Invest your energy wisely. Save your political capital for moments when the stakes are high and the impact on users is significant.

From Contentious Colleague to Unexpected Ally
Finding a Partner When You Need It Most

One moment stands out in my career as a turning point in how I think about workplace relationships, especially with colleagues I did not always see eye to eye with.

I was part of a cross-functional team tasked with reimagining ways to advance human-centered initiatives inside the organization. The assembled team included veterans from design, engineering, operations, and strategy, each of whom held strong opinions and deep expertise. As you might expect with a room full of smart, passionate people, disagreements were frequent and sometimes very heated.

There was one colleague in particular who seemed to be my mirror opposite. We were not adversaries in the personal sense, but our approaches to problem-solving were miles apart. Every discussion turned into a debate. I respected her talent, but it often felt like we were on opposing sides of every argument.

Then came a pivotal meeting. I was presenting a new approach to the group, one I believed could have a big impact on the practice of UX. Most of the people around the table disagreed with me. I expected my usual adversary to join in, but midway through my pitch, she spoke up, not to dismantle my idea, but to support it. She added her own insights, sharpening the case in ways I had not even considered.

I was stunned by her reaction, genuinely speechless. In that moment, the dynamic between us shifted. From that day forward, I saw her not as a barrier, but as someone who could become a powerful ally once we found common ground.

Unless someone is truly toxic, which is rare, disagreement does not make adversaries your enemy. Most of the time, it simply means you have not yet discovered where your interests intersect. Once you do, the colleague you clashed with might turn out to be one of your strongest supporters.

The Lesson: Turning Conflict into Collaboration

I now love it when someone challenges me in a good debate. I cherish opinions that differ from mine and always strive to assemble diverse teams with contrasting backgrounds and perspectives.

Disagreement is inevitable when smart, driven people tackle complex problems together. Colleagues who push us the hardest may be the ones who help us see blind spots, sharpen our thinking, and ultimately strengthen our case.

Call to Action: Build Bridges, Not Walls

Celebrate diversity. Differing perspectives produce better outcomes. Be glad when multiple ideas surface instead of uniform consensus.

Seek first to understand, then to be understood. When someone sees a problem differently from you, probe to understand why. What in their life and work experience has led them to this perspective?

Reframe disagreement. Instead of seeing contentious colleagues as barriers, view them as potential partners who bring valuable perspectives to your argument that you might be missing.

Look for common ground. Even if your approaches differ, take a pause and identify the goals you both share. Use them as a foundation for collaboration.

Fear of Public Speaking
The Essential Skill for Career Advancement

One of the most overlooked skills in UX is teaching. More specifically, it is the ability to communicate your ideas clearly,

persuasively, and confidently in front of an audience. Without this skill, even the sharpest research and the most brilliant design insights can fall flat.

I am an introvert by nature, but my personality shifts when I'm teaching or presenting. Early in my career, though, I was not nearly so confident. My first real presentation opportunity came when a colleague asked me to co-present at a conference. The thought terrified me, but I agreed because my co-presenter was a former professor who knew how to engage an audience. His skill carried us through, and I left the stage both relieved and energized by the experience.

From that point forward, I sought out opportunities to present. I studied how veteran presenters entertained the audience, how they structured their story, and how they ended with a message that inspired.

Over the next few years, I delivered talks at more than a hundred conferences, taught UX training classes inside my companies, and even had the chance to deliver UX presentations to organizations like Microsoft, IBM, and the Economic Development Board of Singapore.

If you can't stand in front of a room of executives and explain, in plain language, what is broken in your product and why it matters, you will never win the support you need to fix it. As a UX professional, your communication and presentation skills are just as important as your wireframes.

The Lesson: Learn from Experts and Keep Practicing

Public speaking is one of the most powerful tools a UX professional can develop. Whether you are standing in front of a conference audience, leading a workshop, or presenting to executives, your effectiveness depends as much on how you communicate as on what you design.

Teaching requires clarity. If you can't explain a concept simply, you probably don't understand it well enough yourself. When colleagues, leaders, or customers see you confidently explain a problem and walk them through a solution, you are not just pitching an idea, you are earning their respect.

But presentation skills don't come naturally. You develop them by watching how seasoned presenters engage an audience, studying what makes stories memorable, and stepping onto the stage again and again.

Call to Action: Add Presentation Skills to Your Goals

Seek out small teaching opportunities. Volunteer to explain a UX principle in a team meeting, walk a stakeholder through a journey map, or present a quick case study.

Co-present with someone experienced. Partnering with a more seasoned speaker gives you a model to learn from and builds confidence before you take the stage alone.

Study great presenters. Search for presentations on YouTube. Pay attention to how they tell stories, use visuals, and keep audiences engaged. Adopt their techniques as your own.

Turn research into stories. Don't just report research findings. Frame them in a way that resonates with your audience's priorities. Help them see the human impact behind the data.

Practice relentlessly. Rehearse your presentations out loud, record yourself, and refine your message. The more comfortable you are with your material, the more space you'll have to read the room and adjust your talk in real time.

Evolving Your Role to Keep Current with Trends
The Shifting Identity of UX

What is in a name? Debates over what we call ourselves—UI, UX, XD, CX, EX, UCD, HCD, UXR, UXD, Design Thinking, Service

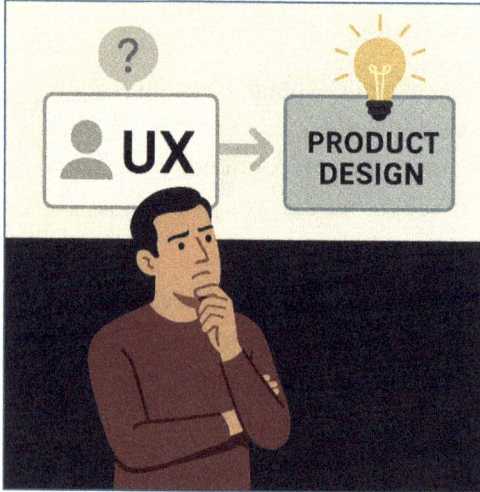

Design, Product Design—have been around for years. Titles multiply, silos form, and too often the signal gets lost in all the noise. What feels like an important distinction to us often looks like needless complexity to our colleagues.

I ran into this problem myself. For several years, I identified as a technical communication manager. That was the title on my business card, and the role I was known for. But when I started job hunting, I discovered there were not many postings for what I thought I was. I ran keyword searches for "technical writing," "documentation," and "communication," but the opportunities were limited.

So I stepped back and asked a question: What do I actually *do* every day?

Over the years, my work had gradually evolved into user experience, including research, interaction design, and content strategy. I just had not changed my title. When I looked at postings for UX managers, they felt like a stretch at first. I wrestled with imposter syndrome. But the responsibilities matched my skills and experience far better than the technical writing roles I had been chasing.

I applied to this new category of job and landed my first role with "UX" in the title.

Now, the cycle is repeating itself. Experience Design is morphing into Product Design, and subdisciplines of UX have split off into separate roles and job titles. In addition, AI is reshaping both UX and content creation at a breathtaking pace. What we do is still mostly the same, but the language, expectations, and skill sets are shifting under our feet.

Jobs evolve, and so must we. Sometimes, staying relevant means rethinking your professional identity before the industry does it for you. It takes a willingness to adapt to the current business climate, but adaptation is both a survival skill and how we grow.

The Lesson: Redefine Yourself Before the Job Market Does

Job titles are temporary. I learned this when I shifted from "technical communication manager" to "UX manager," and it's happening again now with the rise of AI-driven tools.

If you cling tightly to an old title, you risk being left behind, not because your skills are obsolete, but because they are described in a language the market no longer uses. You need to ask whether your current label reflects the work you do or the work the industry now values.

Call to Action: Embrace the Evolution

Audit your professional identity. Don't define yourself with your job title. Instead, write down what you actually do every day, and compare it to the skills the market is demanding right now.

Translate your skills into today's language. The work you have mastered—whether research, writing, design, or strategy—remains valuable, but only if you describe it in terms the industry understands and is hiring for.

Adopt evolving titles. Whether it is Product Design, Experience Design, or something yet to come, remember that labels are temporary. Focus less on what the role is called and more on how your skillset fits into that label.

Overnight Marginalization
A Missed Opportunity Can Sideline You

Sometimes the difference between influence and irrelevance comes down to timing.

A new CEO arrived at my company with a flagship initiative called Total Customer Experience, or TCE. On paper, it was everything I had been advocating for: a holistic view of the customer journey, from first contact through support and beyond. For years, I had been running workshops on end-to-end customer experience, even if we did not yet call it UX, CX, or service design. With the hiring of this new CEO, it seemed the entire organization was about to rally around an idea I deeply believed in.

I was perfectly positioned to be one of the leaders of this program, but because I did not appreciate the politics, I missed the moment.

I should have rebranded my workshop under the TCE banner, broadened its scope to explicitly address each stage of the customer journey, and immediately requested a meeting with the new CEO. I had the expertise, the content, and the timing on my side. With the right framing, I could have positioned myself and UX as a driving force within the initiative.

But I hesitated. While I kept running my sessions as before, the CEO assembled a trusted inner circle of advocates to shape TCE. They became the visible champions, and I found myself drifting to the margins.

I became slowly marginalized, and soon after, I left the company. And while TCE had potential, it never grew into more than a slogan and a slide deck. The opportunity for real culture change was lost, not because the vision was wrong, but because I failed to seize the moment when it was presented to me.

The Lesson: Align Fast and Adopt the New Language

When a new corporate initiative aligns with your area of expertise, don't wait for an invitation to participate. Take the initiative to adapt your work, reframe it in the language of the new strategy, and demonstrate how your contributions can advance its goals.

Seizing moments like this is a critical political strategy. It is essential for ensuring that human-centered thinking is at the table when big changes are being made. If you hesitate, someone less qualified but more politically connected will fill that role, and your chance to influence the outcome may be gone forever.

Call to Action: Don't Miss Your Moment

Build relationships with the initiative's champions. When a new corporate initiative is announced, immediately try to schedule time with sponsors or executives to explain how your expertise can help advance their vision.

Recast the narrative around your work. Speak in the language of new leadership initiatives to illustrate how your work is directly relevant. Adapt your workshops, presentations, and deliverables to reflect support and alignment with the new program.

Ask to contribute. New corporate-wide initiatives usually begin with a working group to iron out the details and formulate a rollout strategy. Volunteer to join the group and explain how your perspectives and influence can help facilitate adoption.

Act now. Hesitation can sideline you. Momentum favors those who step forward first.

Burnout
Losing Your Passion for the Job

After working about four years as a manager, I began to lose my desire to come into work each day. My productivity and my job performance were suffering, and I found myself just sitting at my desk, staring at my computer for hours, achieving nothing. My company used Management by Objectives (similar to OKRs) to track activities and results and each week, I would report to my manager with very few results to show.

I started checking job boards and saw that a new group was hiring for an individual contributor role within a corporate organization that operated as an internal consultancy. The position would have no direct reports, no performance evaluations to write, and no days of back-to-back meetings. It was focused on researching UX best practices, developing new ways to integrate UX into the product lifecycle, and consulting with UX teams across company divisions worldwide.

At first, it seemed like a step backward in my career. I was going from the management position to an individual contributor position, but given my energy level, I really had no choice. Had I continued in my current role, my performance would continue to suffer, probably leading to a layoff. As it turned out, making this move was the best career choice I have ever made.

Throughout my career, I found myself in similar situations. Once I managed a mockup factory where every team member juggled five simultaneous projects—a pace that proved unsustainable. In another role, I worked for years trying to make a difference in my company's UX maturity but was unable to get any traction.

Sometimes, I found a way to re-energize my passion for my job without making a move to a new position. Other times, I changed companies when I felt that my current job was no longer aligned with my career goals. Either way, something had to change.

The Lesson: Burnout Requires Change

Burnout occurs when you become so busy doing your job that you have no time left to work on your mission. Somewhere along the line, the things that you *love* to do diverge from the things that you *have* to do. When this happens, you must rediscover your purpose and make a change. Otherwise, your career will continue on a downward trajectory, during which time you will struggle in vain to do your work every day. Both your work and personal life will suffer, often leading to poor performance evaluations and, ultimately, dismissal.

Call to Action: Rediscover Your Professional Mission

Make a list. Write down all the things you do over the course of a month. Which of these generate energy? Which drain your energy? Imagine your dream job. How far off from your dream job is your current role?

Commit to a passion project. Make time in your schedule to solve for a big unmet customer need, one that is not currently in the product roadmap but needs to be done. Do the research, prototype the solution, and pitch the idea to your leadership.

Move to a new role or a new company. Work with your manager to transition into a new role within your team, one that aligns with what you love to do. Don't be afraid to take a step down. If no new roles are available, start looking for opportunities in other divisions or outside your current company.

Act before it's too late. Taking a vacation is not an answer. If you don't act soon to change your circumstances, your performance will decline, and you will find yourself on a performance improvement plan and vulnerable to the next round of layoffs.

Getting Laid Off
When Competence Becomes a Threat

Based on my experience, I believe it is likely you will be laid off at some point in your career. That kind of rejection always delivers a hit to your self-confidence. But it can actually be a wake-up call that forces you to leave a bad job with the potential for a better one, and will eventually resolve itself into one of the greatest opportunities of your career.

I've been laid off three times, each under very different circumstances:

- Once when a truly incompetent and self-promoting new manager saw a big layoff as a good career move.
- Once when my team was transferred to a new manager who had her own agenda that didn't include me.
- And once when external forces caused our UX work to dry up and the company had no choice but to let me go.

In the aftermath of each situation, I asked myself a series of questions: Could I have prevented it? Could I have played the politics better, protected the team, or found a way to shift perception? Maybe. But the truth is, sometimes competence itself becomes the threat. When leaders don't understand your value—or worse, feel insecure in the presence of your expertise—no amount of diplomacy will change the outcome.

The Lesson: Competence Can Be Threatening

Leadership that doesn't recognize value will eventually discard it.

I took away three lessons from my layoff experiences:

First, recognize when your expertise is unwelcome. If every attempt to add value is met with resistance, defensiveness, or dismissal, you're not in a place where UX can thrive. Don't blame yourself. It's not a reflection of your skill; it's a reflection of financial conditions or mismanagement at the executive level.

Second, know the limits of politics. Building allies, framing UX in business terms, and linking design decisions to financial impact are all essential. But you can't force someone to feel secure in their role. That insecurity belongs to them, not you.

Third, finding a new job can take a long time. Especially now with so much uncertainty around AI, finding your next job can take many months. After I was laid off, it took me eleven months to find a new job. These can be desperate times, but they will get better.

Call to Action: Know When to Move On

Scan for early warning signs. If leadership consistently dismisses your expertise and avoids including you in critical conversations, that's a signal you may be seen as a threat rather than an asset.

Build alliances beyond your chain of command. Seek out product managers, engineers, and mid-level leaders who respect and rely on your work. Strong horizontal support can sometimes offset weak vertical leadership.

Know when it's time to leave. If the culture itself is hostile to UX, no amount of effort will fix it. Protect your team as long as you can, then take your expertise somewhere it will be valued.

Carry layoff lessons forward. Use these experiences to evaluate future opportunities. Ask hard questions about leadership's understanding of UX before joining a new organization, and make sure their commitment to UX matches the impact you want to have.

Quality of Life, Quality of Work
Choosing Between Paycheck and Purpose

Every time we accept a new job, we face a choice: Do we want work that feels meaningful, challenging, and rewarding? Or do we go for the money, because money brings stability, freedom from financial stress, and the ability to improve our quality of life?

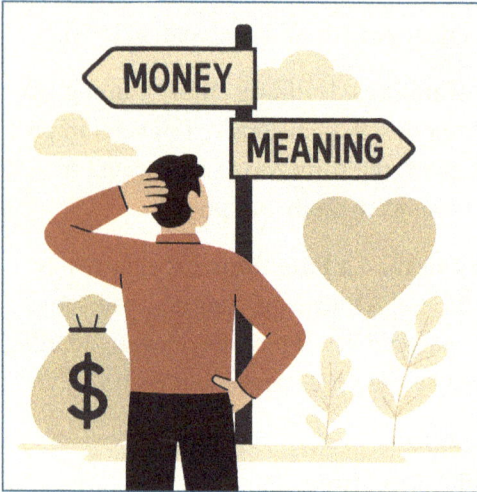

In an ideal world, we would get both. I have been fortunate to land in roles where I was well compensated and doing work that mattered. But there have also been chapters in my career where I had to choose: either stay in a job that paid well but drained my energy, or walk away and look for a job that inspired me but offered less financial security.

There is no right answer. Every UX professional must decide for themselves. I know what it's like to live under financial stress, and I know what it's like to dread going to work every day. Both are miserable in their own way.

My best advice? Don't quit until you have another job lined up. But if you find yourself in a toxic environment, start looking immediately. Be willing to accept less money if the new role gives you back your energy, your creativity, and your sense of purpose—provided the compensation is sufficient to live without constant financial anxiety.

That's what I eventually did. I left a role I did not enjoy for one that was better aligned with my values and my craft. Money matters, but meaningful work matters just as much.

The Lesson: Don't Quit. Plan to Quit.

In the long term, a toxic job with a big paycheck is unsustainable. But following your passion without financial stability creates its own kind of stress. If you don't have both, stay put but start looking for a new job. You will do your best work when you are energized *and* financially secure, and that will translate into long-term career growth.

Call to Action: Plan Your Next Career Move

Don't make a rash decision you'll later regret. Don't walk away in frustration without a plan. No matter how bad your job is, financial stress without a job is worse. It is much safer to line up your next opportunity before leaving your current one. That way, you move into your new job from a position of strength rather than from desperation.

If you're unhappy, you'll probably be laid off anyway. Your performance on the job will suffer, and your unengaged attitude will be noticed. You'll probably be given undesirable assignments and marginalized from important decisions. When you see the signs, step up your search for your next opportunity.

Be willing to take a pay cut. Don't wait for a perfect match in your next employer, one that meets your salary requirements *and* offers interesting work. Sometimes a smaller paycheck buys you a healthier work culture, better teammates, and more energy for life outside work. You can grow your income from there.

Remember that nothing lasts forever. Your next career move will not be your last, so don't demand a perfect balance of income and company culture. As long as you can enjoy your work for the next couple of years, work with good people, and maintain your financial stability, take the job and reassess where you are in a year or two.

Move one rung down the career ladder if you must. I've moved from management to individual contributor and back again. Sometimes this can be your best move.

Advancing the Theory and Practice of UX
UX Must Continue to Evolve and Grow

Most companies will not pay you to rethink the practice of UX itself. They will pay you to deliver the next screen, support the next sprint, or streamline the next workflow. But if you are interested in evolving the craft of UX as I am, you usually have to do that on your own time.

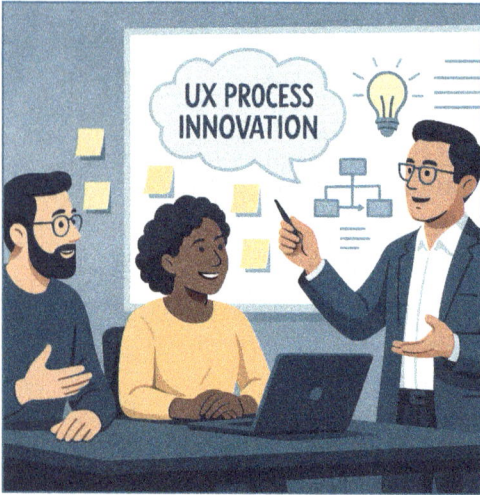

When I speak at conferences, I always begin with the message—"We've come a long way, but we're not there yet"—and close with the entreaty—"Never stop asking, 'What's Next?'" There is still so much to learn and improve how we design and deliver experiences. That's why many years ago I jumped at the chance to join a group called Design for the User, or DFU. Unlike most product-focused UX teams, DFU was a centralized organization with the mission of inventing new ways of practicing UX and raising the company's overall UX maturity.

For a brief window, we had something rare in corporate life. We had time to study industry best practices and to judge whether those practices fit within our company's culture. And we had time to develop pragmatic new methods that worked in our fast-paced, high-stakes environment. In short, we were given the charter of improving the *craft* of UX, not just the application of it.

That luxury does not exist for most teams today, but that doesn't mean you can't make space for it. Maybe not for everyone, and maybe not all the time. But perhaps at least one person on your team can focus on researching and experimenting with new methodologies. If you can't carve out the bandwidth permanently, rotate the role. Let one person explore while others feed the Agile machine. Then allow the next person with a passion project to take over to keep the cycle alive.

The Lesson: Evolve the Practice, Not Just the Product

Process innovation is not optional. It's how we move from "not there yet" to actually getting there. While UX consultants may generate new ideas and methods that move the profession forward, we also need practitioners from inside companies that understand the unique constraints, challenges, and politics of working for an in-house UX team.

If all our energy goes into execution using existing best practices, we will not evolve as a discipline. True progress requires investment in process innovation: streamlining bloated methods, reimagining practices that no longer deliver value, and creating new frameworks that contribute strategically to the business.

Call to Action: Advance the Practice of UX

Carve out space for process innovation. Even if your company will not fund it, create protected time, either an afternoon, a sprint, or a rotating role, for someone on your team—perhaps you?—to explore new ways of practicing UX.

Audit your team's methods. Ask: Which practices consistently deliver value? Which have become rituals with little payoff? Eliminate or adapt the ones that do not serve you.

Prototype new approaches. Treat process changes the same way you treat product design: experiment, test, refine, and validate before scaling.

Translate value into business terms. Show how refining your methods reduces wasted effort, accelerates delivery, or improves outcomes that leaders already care about.

Publish. Share your discoveries and innovations with the rest of us.

Chapter 7: Other Voices, Other Stories

It's important for this book to include stories and perspectives from UX professionals other than my own. This chapter could easily become a multi-volume book series by itself, but for now, I'd like to welcome the contributions of these twelve UX professionals to share episodes and learnings from their careers.

I'm sure their stories will inspire you as much as they have inspired me.

Giselle Daniela Vázquez Chan: UX Under Pressure
Balancing Time, Feasibility, and Usability

When I spoke with a colleague in Argentina, her story echoed many of the patterns I've seen throughout my career. She works

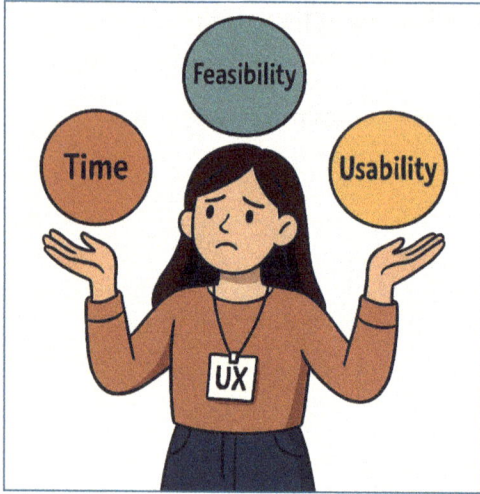

for a bank through a third-party consultancy, focused on onboarding small and medium-sized businesses. Before that, she helped digitize government processes at the national mint. Like many of us, she had freelanced earlier in her career, because quality UX roles were scarce in her region.

She described how process is often determined by the environment. In government, with a tiny development team, everything looked like waterfall. At the bank, the process is "Agile," but in practice it is quarter-by-quarter planning with only rough outlines of what will be built. Features get refined on the fly, and UX is expected to adapt.

Funding for research is minimal. Discovery happens in stolen moments, when developers are tied up with spike tasks. Her UX team is large, but her day-to-day reality is working as a duo inside a feature team. Product owners carry the pressure of keeping developers fully occupied, while UX fights to keep usability on the table.

The biggest challenge, she told me, is balancing three forces: time, technical feasibility, and usability. In that equation, usability almost always comes last. Business priorities and development constraints take precedence, leaving little room for research or exploration. What stops her from practicing UX the way she believes it should be done is not skill or vision. It is timing, investment, and the relentless pressure to deliver now.

The Lesson: Usability Always Risks Coming Last

What her story reveals is a truth many UX professionals know too well. Business and technology often dominate the decision-making process, while usability is treated as optional. Research is underfunded, discovery is squeezed into the margins, and user needs are refined only after business and technical decisions are locked in.

UX maturity is not just about methods or team size. It is about whether usability is treated as an equal partner. When it isn't, the result is predictable: solutions that meet deadlines and technical requirements but leave customers struggling.

Call to Action: Protect the Role of Usability

Push for balance. Remind stakeholders that business viability, technical feasibility, and usability must work together. Without usability, the other two will not sustain.

Make research visible. Even small discoveries—shared as clips, quotes, or simple prototypes—can highlight gaps and reframe priorities.

Use timing strategically. Capture opportunities when developers are occupied or when features are loosely defined. Even small inputs at the right moment can redirect outcomes.

Challenge assumptions. When someone says, "We already know what users want," counter with evidence, however modest.

Timothy Chan: Evidence Meets Resistance
Designing Under Fire

Early in my career, a developer recruited me to help fix what he described as a "disaster" of a platform. He was right. The product

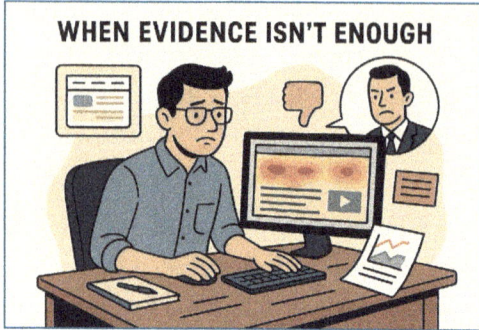

was chaotic, with no quality assurance, no prioritization, and engineers responding to the loudest customer request by coding it immediately and pushing it live. By the time I arrived, the interface had ballooned into thirteen horizontal tabs, and customer service was flooded with complaints. Nothing was findable, and basic tasks took ten clicks.

I knew we needed evidence to change minds. I introduced Hotjar to capture analytics and highlight where users were struggling. This data became my lifeline with the engineering-focused CTO, who believed UX was slowing things down and that the quickest path was always to just add more code. At first, he dismissed my input, but once I showed him heatmaps and session recordings, he started to listen, at least for small fixes.

To go further, I pushed for a local UX researcher who could speak directly with customers. Her discovery work uncovered not only what users struggled with but also why. Together, we showed the cost of patchwork fixes and the value of thoughtful design. Slowly, user feedback scores rose from 1.9 to 3.5. Developers embraced the design system I created because I had built it with their input. For a while, it felt like we were turning the tide.

But progress always stalled at the CTO's desk. He once told me research should take no more than three hours. Even after other executives supported us, he doubled down: "No research. No roadmaps. Just ship the code." Within a month, the entire UX team was laid off.

That was crushing, not just professionally but personally. I had seen customers relieved when friction disappeared. I knew their stress would return as the product regressed. What I learned was sobering: methods, data, and design systems can only take you so far. If leadership views UX as an obstacle instead of a driver of value, no amount of evidence will change their mind.

It taught me that UX is not just about advocating for users, it is also about navigating organizational politics. And sometimes, despite your best efforts, the culture will not change. When that happens, the most important decision is knowing when to move on.

The Lesson: Fighting for UX on Hostile Ground

This experience reinforced for me that UX maturity is not just about methods, it is about politics. Evidence, research, and design systems matter, but they do not guarantee influence. If leadership views UX as a blocker rather than a driver of value, progress stalls no matter how strong the case. The real challenge is not only building better experiences for users but also navigating organizational dynamics: knowing when to push, when to adapt, and when to recognize that change may not be possible under a given leader.

I also learned that incremental wins, such as improved feedback scores or developers embracing a design system, can only carry a team so far if executive buy-in is absent. The most frustrating moments came not from the complexity of the design problems but from watching genuine improvements get dismissed as slowing things down. That is when you realize UX success requires more than technical skill. It requires advocacy, diplomacy, and sometimes the courage to walk away when the environment can't sustain the work.

Finally, I was reminded of why UX matters so deeply. When customers saw improvements, they were relieved. Their stress decreased. They felt heard. Those reactions are why we do this work. And when leadership undermines that mission, the people who truly lose are the users. For me, that was the hardest part: knowing we had made life better for them, only to watch the progress disappear.

Call to Action: Turning Evidence into Influence

Gather evidence early. Use analytics, customer feedback, or tools like Hotjar to ground your case in data before pushing for design changes. Evidence builds credibility, especially with skeptical leaders.

Anticipate politics. Recognize that resistance may not come from the quality of your work but from leadership priorities, power dynamics, or personality clashes. Plan your strategy accordingly.

Frame UX as acceleration, not obstacle. Translate improvements into business outcomes such as reduced support calls, faster workflows, and higher satisfaction, so leaders see UX as speeding progress, not slowing it down.

Celebrate incremental wins. Share stories and results that show how small UX improvements reduce user stress and drive measurable gains. These moments keep morale high and strengthen advocacy.

Build allies across functions. Partner with developers, product managers, and customer service teams who can echo user pain points and support UX priorities when leadership is resistant.

Know when to move on. Sometimes the environment simply will not support UX maturity. Recognize the signs, preserve your energy, and seek out organizations that value and enable the work.

Chuck Griffith: The Insight That Bombed
Knowing When and Where to Speak Truth to Power

The room was already full when I arrived. One of those conference rooms with no windows, just dry-erase walls and a pricing web page projected in the front. Product marketing leadership squatted the front rows, their SVP at the head of the table, laptops open. I took an empty seat near the back, notebook open, pen ready.

He commanded the room naturally. When he made a joke, they laughed. When he gestured, they nodded. I watched the choreography from the only remaining seat, right behind him.

He started tossing out changes to the page. Make the "Contact Sales" button larger. Move the feature comparison higher. Add the enterprise tier above the fold instead of below. Each suggestion landed with enthusiasm. A few others lobbed questions, and he fielded them smoothly, clicking through sections of the page.

Every idea was familiar. My team had tested them all over the past six months: hundreds of users, dozens of prototypes, clear data. The results weren't subtle.

By his third suggestion, I couldn't stay quiet. We'd spent six months testing pricing pages across our cloud products, and I knew most of his ideas would waste time and effort.

I spoke. "We tested that button size last quarter. The larger version performed well on clicks but reduced conversions."

The SVP nodded without looking back. "Good to know," he said, already scrolling to the next section.

At that point, I thought he hadn't heard me clearly.

He suggested moving the comparison table. I answered again. "That one didn't move the needle either. Users ignored it in that position."

A few heads turned. Someone shifted in their chair. He proposed leading with the enterprise tier. I interrupted once more. "We tried that in three variations. Every version increased bounce rate and reduced form completions."

In my world, this kind of exchange was normal. Surely the research spoke for itself.

He didn't look up from his screen. His team stayed quiet, polite smiles fixed. The easy rhythm of the meeting gave way to stillness. I'm still not sure why I kept going. Each time I spoke, the silence stretched a little longer.

Finally, he stopped scrolling. He closed his laptop and turned, the movement slow, deliberate. The room froze.

He smiled. Not a warm smile. A professional one. Precise. "Thank you for being so insightful," he said. "I really appreciate it."

The pause hung in the room. I mistook it for approval. The tension left my shoulders. For a few seconds, I thought I'd earned a small win.

When the meeting ended, I gathered my things. A few people thanked him on their way out. No one spoke to me. I told myself they were distracted, that everyone was thinking about next steps.

Back at my desk, I replayed the scene. The pause. The smile. The way his whole body had turned to face me. My gut told me something hadn't played right, but I wasn't sure why.

Halfway through a rushed commissary lunch at my desk, a coworker from his team appeared. She worked in strategy; we'd partnered before and she felt like an ally.

"That line," she said quietly. "'...insightful?' You know he was trying to shut you down."

I sat there long after the office emptied, contemplating whether I should pour a glass of beer from the kitchen keg and draft an email apologizing.

I'd dismantled his flow in front of everyone, turning a momentum-building session into a usability report. I hadn't asked what they'd explored or why they were revisiting these changes. Maybe he already knew the test results and was using the conversation to bring his team to a decision he'd already made.

It's a pet peeve of mine when people "solution in the room," but I realized I hadn't questioned the problem he was trying to solve.

My mistake was in the delivery. His team lost face in front of their boss. The correction felt public, not collaborative. I was an invited guest in someone else's forum. I had expertise, but not jurisdiction.

The signals came quietly. Fewer invites from his group. Polite emails. Short hallway exchanges. Nothing direct, but unmistakable.

A few weeks later, when I led my own design review, a junior researcher interrupted to challenge a key wireframe. My first reaction was defensiveness, the same flash I'd once seen on the SVP's face. Then memory caught up to me. The pause. The smile. The silence that followed.

I stopped the meeting. I thanked him again in front of the team to reinforce that curiosity is welcome and to apply what I'd learned from the SVP *about what not to do.*

The Lesson: Build Trust Before Offering Public Feedback

Expertise doesn't equal influence. People hear truth only when they feel safe hearing it. Authority depends on timing, respect, and awareness of context. Before offering corrections, know who owns the room. Recognize when you're a guest in someone else's space. Choose when to teach, when to listen, and when to wait. Influence means knowing when your voice strengthens the room and when it fractures it.

I came to understand that influence means pulling back from what you know and leaning into others' curiosity. Ask what's been explored and why before just citing data and research.

Call to Action: Lay the Foundation for Critique

Build private trust before public correction. If you have contradictory data, share it afterward in a one-on-one. Frame it as support, not challenge. Give leaders room to integrate your findings without losing credibility.

Praise what works before suggesting changes. Acknowledge the purpose behind a design before surfacing its flaws. People protect what they build. Honor that instinct.

Understand that some meetings are about momentum, not discovery. Some exist to create consensus or alignment. If you misread the goal, your research becomes interference.

Read the room's hierarchy. Notice who speaks freely and who waits to be prompted. Observe body language. Track who interrupts and who commands silence. Pay attention to the invisible jurisdiction that defines belonging.

Wait to be invited before offering expertise. If you're in another leader's forum, your role is to strengthen their narrative, not replace it. Cross-functional influence means reading lines that aren't written on an org chart.

Insight lands best when it respects the moment and the people holding the decision.

Carlos Martínez Domínguez: Fighting for Research in a Startup
When Product Owns UX

When I stepped into a new leadership role at a startup, I quickly realized how fragile the company's approach to design really was.

Service design is meant to understand the end-to-end experience, but here everything was built on assumptions. Product managers would casually declare, "If I were the user, I'd want this feature to do X or Y." I had to keep reminding them: "You're not the user. We need to do research."

My first move was to hire UX researchers. We were just six people—two researchers, a UX designer, a UI designer, and a graphic designer—but it was enough to start shifting the culture. Convincing the product team, though, was an uphill climb. They saw research as wasted time, something that slowed down development. I tried to show them another way: "Let's intertwine the work. While you're developing one sprint, we'll run discovery. By the time you finish, we'll have insights to guide the next iteration." But the pushback was relentless: "It takes too long." "We already know what users want."

I even escalated to the CEO, explaining that a bit of research upfront would save us from costly rework later. He listened politely, but his mantra was speed. The result was predictable: we kept skipping discovery, only to find ourselves patching problems after launch.

Despite resistance, our researchers pressed ahead. One mapped the customer journey beyond the product, looking at how people accomplished tasks today, not just how they used our tool. Another spent two months tracing the end-to-end experience of an online valuation product, then worked with sales reps to create richer user profiles.

In another instance, we helped improve satisfaction for people requesting a property valuation. By interviewing users, mapping their journey, and understanding the mental model of sellers, we improved the experience of asking for an estimate in meaningful ways.

The acquisitions team saw the value immediately; satisfaction scores ticked upward. But with the product team, it was always the same refrain: "Too complicated. Not invented here."

The deeper issue wasn't process; it was territory. The head of product wasn't used to design leadership existing outside his domain. Every time we brought evidence, he countered with "If I were the user…" And with the CEO backing speed over strategy, the pattern held. Eventually, after some quick wins, our team was dissolved in a round of layoffs.

The real friction with product showed most clearly when we proposed changes to the value proposition of two key products. Users found them confusing, and our research suggested splitting them into three distinct products with added features to better match user needs and decision-making. That's when product felt we were "invading" their space, and the pushback ultimately led to design being sidelined in the startup.

Looking back, I see it as a cultural impasse. We proved research could improve experiences. We showed measurable gains. But product wanted ownership of UX, and leadership saw no value in slowing down. Sometimes design simply can't win the political battle.

The Lesson: When Politics Overshadows UX

This experience taught me that UX maturity is not defined by methods, talent, or even results. It is defined by politics. We built a capable team, ran research that uncovered real customer pain points, and even improved satisfaction scores. But evidence alone wasn't enough. Without leadership buy-in, progress hit a wall.

The head of product viewed UX as territory, not as a discipline with its own value. That mindset undermined collaboration and prevented meaningful change. The CEO, driven by speed, reinforced the same message: new features mattered more than customer understanding. In that environment, even small fixes became uphill battles.

I learned that UX success depends as much on organizational structure as it does on skill. Reporting lines matter. Who owns UX matters. And the willingness of leaders to see design as a driver of value, not just a delivery function, matters most of all.

The hard truth is that sometimes politics outweighs progress. Incremental wins can keep a team motivated, but without executive support they rarely stick. When UX is seen as a threat instead of a partner, the work risks being undone no matter how strong the evidence.

The deeper lesson is one of resilience. As UX professionals, we must build allies, advocate persistently, and frame our work in business terms leaders understand. But we also have to recognize when an environment simply can't sustain UX maturity. In those cases, the most courageous act may be to step away and find a place where design is valued, not sidelined.

Call to Action: Navigating UX Politics

Gather evidence early. Collect analytics, customer feedback, or observational research before proposing changes. Data provides credibility when opinions clash.

Frame UX in business terms. Translate user insights into outcomes leaders value such as reduced support costs, faster workflows, and higher adoption. Show UX as an accelerator, not an obstacle.

Build allies across functions. Partner with developers, product managers, and customer service teams. When multiple voices echo the same user pain points, it's harder for leadership to ignore.

Document tradeoffs. If compromises are made, record them. This protects the UX team from blame later and highlights the long-term costs of short-term decisions.

Celebrate incremental wins. Share stories and metrics that highlight progress, even small ones. These wins keep morale high and remind the organization of UX's value.

Recognize when to move on. Not every culture can sustain UX maturity. If leadership consistently treats UX as a threat or unnecessary overhead, it may be time to find a place that values your craft.

Vivian Gomes: Building Human-Centered Design in India

Bridging Cultures, Breaking Barriers, Centering Humanity

When I began working in India in 2001, the idea of usability and user-centered design was virtually unknown. The culture was

simple: do not ask questions, just do as directed. I had just come from a company with an open, creative culture, so the resistance I encountered was jarring.

I was hired into a small advanced technology group by the CPO, who believed new, future-focused businesses could drive revenue. My role was to create go-to-market kits. What was supposed to take a year, I completed in two and a half months. When she asked what I wanted to do next, I said I wanted to start a design center in India. She agreed, but then announced she was quitting. Her replacement, a rocket scientist, admitted he knew nothing about usability but supported me in launching a new service. Within three months, he was gone.

Left without a leader, I pushed forward anyway. A program manager in San Diego connected me to a project and gave me $10,000 to set up a usability lab in China. With almost no budget, we partnered with a university: we would build their lab, and in return, borrow it for a month. That scrappy effort produced research that changed everything. We shifted one of our products from a maze of hardware buttons to a touch screen, cutting call rates to nearly zero and generating $270 million in two quarters.

From there, my India team grew to 35, funded from San Diego but resisted locally. My managers in India wanted no part of what we were doing. But by forging alliances, especially with HR, we began to support teams across Singapore, Shanghai, Barcelona, and beyond. Over four years, we delivered research and design to 13 countries.

The resistance eventually wore me down, and I left to form my own company, Human Factors Research & Design. Ironically, my former employer became my first client.

That experience taught me a crucial distinction: UX design can produce elegant interfaces, but without a human-centered foundation it risks missing the bigger picture. Tools have always been extensions of human capabilities that enable new achievements. Our work is to ensure design evolves with humanity at the center. That is what I carried into my consulting practice, teaching human-centered design and embedding it directly into organizations so they could sustain it themselves.

The Lesson: UX Without Humanity Falls Short

My journey made one truth unmistakably clear: UX alone is not enough. A sleek interface or efficient workflow can still fail if it is disconnected from the deeper human context. True impact comes when design does not just optimize screens but reimagines how technology extends human capability.

I learned that resistance is inevitable when introducing new disciplines, especially in cultures where questioning leadership is discouraged. Persistence, alliances, and creative workarounds such as building a usability lab in exchange for access can open doors that budgets and org charts will not. But the real breakthrough happens when research connects directly to business outcomes. Moving a product from buttons to touch screens did not just improve usability. It saved a failing product and generated hundreds of millions in revenue. That kind of result silences skeptics.

I also discovered that while UX can evolve inside organizations, it thrives when anchored in a human-centered philosophy. UX is the craft; human-centered design is the compass. Without that compass, organizations risk building beautiful tools that nobody truly needs.

Finally, I learned that influence often means speaking in the language others value: ROI, efficiency, and revenue while never losing sight of the human story. That balance is what sustained my practice long after the internal politics pushed me out.

Call to Action: From UX to Human-Centered Design

Research beyond the product. Do not just ask how people use your product. Study how they accomplish their goals without it. That is where the real opportunities for impact live.

Analyze through a human lens. Translate findings into insights about people, not just screens. Focus on needs, motivations, and pain points that shape the experience.

Visualize outcomes, not just interfaces. Create models and stories that show how lives improve, not only how UIs look.

Engage leaders through business impact. Tie design recommendations to metrics that matter such as ROI, retention, efficiency, and revenue while keeping the human story front and center.

Measure what matters. Track both business outcomes and human outcomes. Reducing call center volume is as important as reducing customer frustration.

Repeat relentlessly. Human needs evolve, technologies shift, and organizations reorganize. Keep pushing for research, analysis, and storytelling that connect UX back to humanity.

Ariel Grace Snapp: Navigating Business Motivations
Timing, Politics, and the UX Tightrope

When I first entered the field, UX was still in its infancy. At one of my earliest jobs, I quickly learned that not everyone in business was an empath or thought about the customer. That was a hard lesson. At one of my jobs, for instance, the company was in the middle of a massive digital transformation, shifting from hardware to software and digital communications. The global UX team existed, but many members were transitioning from industrial design and struggled to adapt to Agile and Lean practices. It felt like moving a tanker: progress was possible, but painfully slow.

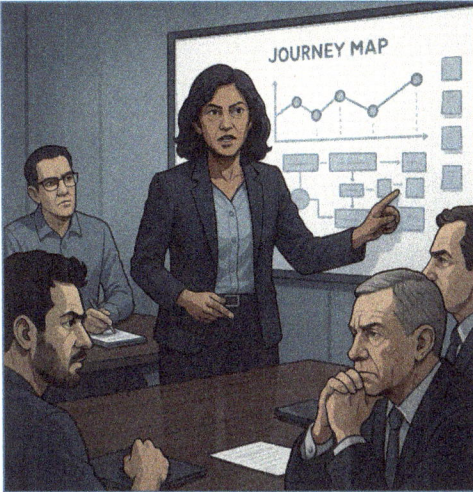

I have often gravitated toward the innovation side of UX, which comes with its own risks. At one company, an executive poured millions into a bold new idea that ultimately failed simply because the timing was not right. He lost his job, and I was left reflecting on how vision alone is not enough. Timing matters. Markets matter. And sometimes you can see exactly where things need to go but can't drag an organization there at the pace you want.

One of the most intense experiences came when I was brought in to rescue a failing project. They had not done a single round of user research. Internal consultants had hired an external development shop, but things were collapsing. The stakes were high, lawsuits loomed in the background, and I walked straight into the C-suite on day one.

Those meetings were tense. Stakeholders were angry, defensive, and deeply invested in their own agendas. Human-centered framing helped shift the conversation, but talking directly to customers was off the table. I had to be pragmatic, working with the product leader to consolidate forty disparate tools while quietly sneaking user-centric methods into the process.

Setting boundaries was essential. They wanted me to solve everything on day one but I had to say no. We needed a team, and we needed to do this the right way. I remember one heated meeting where a developer stormed out over something as small as a login flow. It was a stark reminder that UX challenges are rarely about the design itself—they are about politics, power, and change.

What I have learned through all of this is that UX is never just about wireframes or prototypes. It is about timing, diplomacy, and persistence. You fight for research, you frame it in ways leadership can accept, and sometimes you accept that even good ideas will fail if the organization is not ready.

The Lesson: UX Is as Much Politics as Practice

The longer I have worked in UX, the clearer it has become that success depends as much on navigating people and politics as it does on methods and tools. Evidence, research, and design craft only go so far if the organization isn't ready or willing to change.

I have learned that timing matters. Even the best ideas can fall flat if a company isn't prepared to embrace them. Patience, relationship-building, and shared language are just as critical as wireframes or research findings. Transformation isn't about convincing everyone overnight; it is about steadily creating openings and seizing the moments when leadership is willing to listen.

I have also learned that pragmatism is essential. Sometimes, introducing UX in small, accessible ways such as story mapping or reframing business goals in human-centered terms can open doors that direct customer research or bold design proposals would slam shut. The key is to meet organizations where they are, not where you wish they were.

Finally, I have learned that resistance is rarely about the work itself. It is about fear, politics, and priorities. By anticipating those dynamics, framing UX in terms that resonate with stakeholders, and documenting compromises, UX leaders can protect their teams and preserve momentum.

Call to Action: Design for Politics as Much as Products

Map the landscape. Before pushing for change, identify the motivations, fears, and priorities of stakeholders. Knowing the political terrain is as critical as knowing the user journey.

Frame in their language. Translate UX insights into business terms. Tie research to metrics, usability to revenue, and design improvements to efficiency. Speak the language that resonates with leadership.

Start small, build trust. Introduce approachable practices such as highlights reels or simple prototypes. Small wins demonstrate value without triggering resistance.

Document tradeoffs. When compromises are forced, record them. Create a paper trail that protects the UX team and shows how decisions impact outcomes.

Time your push. Look for organizational inflection points such as leadership changes, major initiatives, or crises when openness to new approaches is highest.

Balance patience with persistence. Culture change moves slowly. Stay pragmatic, build allies, and know when to push harder and when to wait.

Jacqui Miller: Building Research Communities
Research-Resistant Organizations

When I first began working with technology companies, I expected them to be more advanced in UX maturity. What I found

was often the opposite: organizations caught between startup chaos and the discipline of becoming a full-fledged company.

At one firm, I joined just as they were setting up a UX team. It was an exciting moment, but leadership squabbles undermined progress. When the leader who had championed our work left, the entire effort collapsed. At the next company, a fintech, the situation was even worse. UX research was treated as a checkbox. Talking to real customers, I was told, was not necessary. "We are the users," they insisted.

Today, I am in a company where design is considered mature, and I am building the UX research group from the ground up. But even here, roadblocks are constant. Many PMs still see research as validation only, and some barely understand what research means. I have been vocal about integrating research into every part of the process. To do this, I built a research panel and pushed for visibility on our customer-facing site. It felt like overhead work, but it was essential groundwork to get real users into the room.

The turning point came during our first workshop. We invited a small group of customers, and when PMs heard them speak candidly, you could see the synapses firing. Suddenly the abstract "user" was real. They asked eagerly when we could do the next one. That moment was pivotal for building momentum.

Still, the politics are complex. Sales teams, deeply connected to customers, push hard for fixes. PMs, wary of conflict, resist involving them. I constantly remind everyone: "Don't pretend you know what the users want. Connect me to them so I can gather real data."

Workshops became our bridge. We kept them small, no more than eight participants, and sometimes had to turn people away. Customers were so eager that some even paid their own way to attend. The magic happened when large and small companies shared practices with one another. A learning community began to form, with insights spreading organically.

For me, the biggest myth I have fought is that "all our customers are different." Their contexts vary, but their goals are the same. Whether in pharma or IT, they want reliability, clarity, and resilience. By focusing on those shared outcomes, we have been able to cut through politics and make progress, slowly but meaningfully.

The Lesson: Building a Research Culture Against the Odds

What I learned through these experiences is that UX research isn't just about gathering data. It is about creating momentum. Evidence matters, but the real breakthrough often comes when stakeholders see and hear customers directly. A well-designed workshop can do more to change minds in a few hours than months of slide decks.

Another lesson is that infrastructure matters. Panels, processes, and communication channels may not look like "research," but without them, research can't scale. Building those foundations creates continuity that outlasts individual projects.

Finally, the most powerful insight is that customers, regardless of their industry or context, share more common goals than differences. By bringing them together, patterns emerge that not only inform better products but also build a sense of community among users themselves. That shared learning creates trust, loyalty, and a natural feedback loop that fuels continuous improvement.

Invest in community, not just studies. Research isn't a one-way street. When customers teach each other and shape the product alongside you, the value multiplies—for them, for your company, and for the discipline of UX.

Call to Action: Turning Research into a Community

Invest in infrastructure. Build the systems that support research so insights don't get lost and participation scales over time.

Create shared experiences. Don't just collect data. Design workshops and sessions where stakeholders hear customers firsthand. The emotional impact of these encounters builds empathy and accelerates buy-in.

Mix perspectives. Bring together diverse customers, both large and small, experienced and new. Their conversations reveal patterns and best practices that no one group could surface alone.

Make research a habit. Schedule recurring workshops and engagements so learning is continuous. Treat these sessions as part of the development rhythm, not as one-off events.

Amplify customer voices. Capture and share customer stories in ways that developers, PMs, and executives can act on. Evidence is more compelling when it is tied to real human experiences.

Build a learning community. Encourage customers to share what they have discovered with each other. When users learn from one another, your research impact multiplies, and so does customer loyalty.

Zack Naylor: Don't Fight Fire with Fire
Educating Stakeholders on the Value of Research

I was once part of a team working on the mobile app of a national fitness company. This was one of many products and services

offered by this organization. At the time I joined the team, I had been in this new role for, at most, three months. There was an existing team of designers working on the mobile app, both very talented and one of them also very senior, having worked at the company for

seven or eight years at the time.

Stakeholders came to them asking for a "new home screen." Now, these folks already working on the mobile app were very much product designers. My role, however, spanned across business discovery, user research, strategy, and design. So, when I got assigned to help with this effort, my "Spidey sense" tingled at the request for a new home screen design. Anyone who's been in UX for more than a few years has an intuition for things like this that there's often a deeper need and an unspoken request that's not being expressed (or not fully understood…yet!).

To make things even trickier, the relationship between design and the business (specifically the Director of the mobile app and the VP of Digital Marketing—both primary owners and stakeholders for the mobile app) was not great. In one meeting, I witnessed the most senior designer working to suggest potential changes that addressed deeper needs—not just a new home screen—and the VP of Digital Marketing took a blank sheet of paper, drew a new home screen with a few navigation items, and turned to them saying "just design this." Not a great demonstration of trust and collaboration.

So naturally, in the next meeting with myself and those two designers, I suggested we redesign the entire app navigation. No, I'm not kidding. Yes, of course, the designers thought I was mad and told me the stakeholders would never go for it. I told them "Hey, I'm the 'new guy' here and if it doesn't work, you can 100% blame me, but if it does…well then we'd have just designed a 180-degree improvement for this failing mobile app".

I immediately scheduled separate one-on-one meetings with the Director of the Mobile App and the VP of Digital Marketing to understand their needs—both personal and business-related—for this mobile app. We talked about the need a new home screen would solve, why the business had a mobile app, etc.

The very next meeting, there was great discussion about how to move forward after we shared a high-level prototype for the suggested changes (which were significantly more than just a home screen refresh). The tone of the conversation shifted from accusatory to exploratory. After convincing the team that we ought to get these concepts in front of actual customers, we were off.

I ran a handful of lightweight, in-person usability tests on a clickable prototype to gather data and help confirm direction for next steps.

In the very next meeting, including the stakeholders, we had the entire team accept every design change and recommendation we proposed. The app went on to receive a five-star rating in the next few months.

The Lesson: Learn from Stakeholders As You Would Customers

By truly listening to stakeholders, sharing a genuine interest in their stake in it personally as well as how this product helped the company, I was able to demonstrate that my perspective and suggested changes were directly informed by the goals of the business. It was no longer about one person's opinion vs another's. First seek to understand, then to be understood.

Call to Action: Understand the Business, Early and Often

Conduct stakeholder interviews. Now. Seriously, schedule them as soon as possible. Have conversations with the business folks and stakeholders who are ultimately responsible for the success of the product or service you're working on. Not only will you gain trust, but you'll identify key drivers to address in your next conversation and working sessions.

Create a shared language. By having gathered a ton of good information about what the business is hoping to accomplish, you can formulate a shared set of goals, using language that cross-functional teams can understand.

Tie your recommendations directly to business goals. With goals established along with a shared language to discuss those goals, you're now equipped to propose new features, design changes, and recommendations…all directly tied to how they will help the company meet the goals that everyone agreed to. No more "fights"—just conversations about the best way to win, together.

Karthikeyan Panneerselvam: From Saying "No" to Making It Real
The Politics of UX Leadership

When I stepped into my new role, I inherited chaos: five product managers, five conflicting priorities, and no single leader to unify

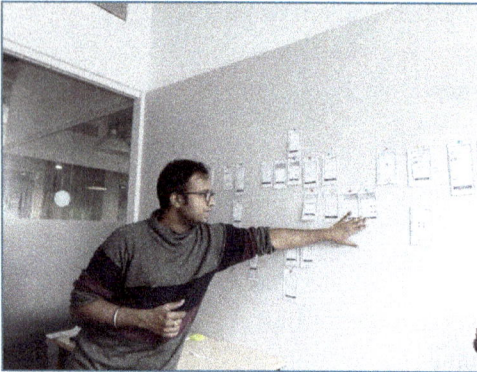

them. Everyone came directly to design with requests, often underestimating the effort. A "quick change" was assumed to be two hours of work, with developers and PMs casually guessing at UX effort.

At first, I said yes too often. The cost was my peace of mind—and my sleep.

The turning point came when the CEO personally asked me to take on a new project. I looked at my overstretched team and said no. He was disappointed enough to escalate to the founders. But that "no" finally forced a real conversation about priorities. Ironically, it created alignment that months of "yes" had failed to deliver.

From Jargon to JIRA

I also realized that framing mattered as much as boundaries. When I introduced frameworks like the Double Diamond, people listened politely but didn't connect. PMs and engineers weren't interested in "information hierarchy" or "architecture." The only thing they cared about was:

"When will the design be ready?"

So, I stopped teaching theory and reframed design in the language everyone already used: JIRA.

I broke the process into four clear stages (interestingly, since it starts with 0 so the 4 steps actually sounded like 3 steps):

- **D0: Problem.** Define the business problem, user needs, and tech constraints.
- **D1: Solution.** Broad brush strokes—happy path flows, wireframes, success metrics.
- **D2: Functionality.** Secondary and negative cases, information hierarchy, behavioral metrics.
- **D3: Aesthetics.** Once function was clear, refine visuals—color, typography, brand story. This step was optional if we successfully build the design system. More reasons for me to get the budget approval for hiring a design system expert because all stakeholders wanted to remove the D3 step completely.

For the few curious PMs, this sequencing made design easier to understand. For everyone else, it kept things simple: instead of vague jargon, they could just ask *"Are we at D1 or D3?"*

The Payoff

The effect was immediate. "In progress" no longer felt like a black box. Stakeholders could see where design stood without a lecture in UX theory.

The validation came when a delayed project escalated. My manager—who was not a designer—called me and asked:

"When can I get D3 for this project?"

That question told me the process had landed. Design was no longer seen as vague artistry. It had become a department with structure, milestones, and credibility.

The Lesson: The Power of Saying No

UX leadership isn't about saying yes to everything. Real influence comes from setting boundaries and making design understandable to the organization. Sometimes that means saying no to the CEO. Sometimes it means turning the Double Diamond into D0–D3 on a JIRA board.

Either way, the politics of UX is about clarity—so that even non-designers start asking for "D3." That's when you know design has become real.

Call to Action: Master the Politics

Say No to Create Yes. Boundaries force clarity on priorities.

Translate, Don't Preach. Theory inspires designers, but pragmatism earns trust.

Make Progress Visible. Clear stages turn "in progress" into something tangible.

Design as a Department. Structure shifts perception from craft to capability.

Scott Parker: The Politics of Agile and UX
From Silos to Shared Outcomes

When our company merged with another organization, we brought the teams together through our centralized partnership, giving us a single UX function. Designers were embedded into scrum teams but remained connected as a functional team and unified practice. A sound foundation, but the politics quickly surfaced.

Product teams wanted to "own" designers outright. They argued for full-time resources dedicated to their slice of the business, often forgetting that no single designer could be a unicorn who handled everything. Our model was built on shared skills, with each designer leaning on the wider team for specialized support. That did not sit well with some. They pushed for control, insisting that their priorities mattered most, even when it fragmented the overall user experience.

We needed to bring them round, to counter the fragmentation. Teams optimized for their own area, with little regard for the ecosystem. We championed consistency, reminding everyone that optimizing one corner at the expense of the whole creates disruption. But competing strategies, KPIs, and OKRs often overpowered the broader vision.

Agile added another layer of tension. Developers insisted on high-fidelity screens for every story, turning design into a bottleneck. Some in the cross-functional teams—and beyond—were overly confident—they "knew the users" because they used technology themselves. Instead of validating assumptions with research, they leaned on anecdote. UX was cast as slowing things down.

We tried to counter this with transparency. We introduced research playbacks, shared participant criteria, and even provided raw video so teams could see firsthand how users responded. We framed ourselves not as gatekeepers but as facilitators of evidence. Slowly, credibility grew, though it was hard-won.

The deeper problem was cultural. Agile had been introduced, with some people having "purist" attitudes and the absence of UX in the origin of Agile was felt strongly. Our core users didn't want regular updates disrupting their workflows. Our release cadence had to align with their natural cycles, not just our sprints. But that nuance rarely made it into planning conversations.

At the heart of it all was the politics of ownership: who controlled priorities, who defined research, and who got credit for the work. For UX to succeed, we had to constantly rebalance power, championing outcomes over features, pushing for collaboration over silos, and insisting on a holistic experience even when the organization wanted shortcuts.

The Lesson: Balancing Politics, Process, and People

What this experience reinforced is that UX success is not just about design craft. It is about navigating the politics of ownership. Product managers, developers, and executives all bring their own priorities, incentives, and egos into the process. If they "own" UXers directly, the work gets fragmented and the broader ecosystem suffers. Centralizing UX as a cohesive practice helps protect against that, but it also requires constant negotiation and diplomacy.

Agile can amplify these tensions. Without careful integration, UX is cast as a bottleneck, slowing down sprints instead of enabling better outcomes. That is a false narrative. By being transparent with research, sharing raw evidence, and framing improvements in terms of business impact, we can gradually build credibility. Still, credibility is not enough on its own. UX has to fight for the right balance: protecting holistic experience while adapting to the rhythms of the business and its customers.

The larger lesson is this: methods and frameworks matter, but politics and power dynamics shape whether UX thrives or stalls. If you want to protect the user experience, you must also protect the conditions that allow it to flourish: team structure, credibility, timing, and shared ownership. Without that foundation, even the best design intentions risk being swallowed by organizational silos.

Call to Action: Protect the Conditions for UX to Thrive

Centralize UX as a cohesive practice. Ensure UX reports into a unified function, a centralised partnership rather than being scattered under product or engineering. This protects against fragmented experiences and builds organizational credibility.

Push back against "ownership" of designers. Reframe the conversation away from individuals being "dedicated resources" toward shared access to the breadth of UX skills across the team.

Champion outcomes over features. Shift roadmaps from "what are we building" to "what problems are we solving." Use customer stories and research evidence to make the case for focusing on impact.

Be transparent with research. Share methods, participant criteria, and even raw data when possible. Transparency disarms skepticism and helps build trust across product and engineering.

Adapt to business rhythms. Recognize when customers can and cannot absorb changes. Advocate for release cadences that align with user realities, not just developer velocity.

Balance diplomacy with advocacy. Work with product managers and developers as partners, not rivals. But do not shy away from reminding stakeholders that without a cohesive UX perspective, the customer experience will fracture.

Jigar Tewar: Two Worlds of Design
Service vs. Product

Over the years, I've had the chance to work in both service design and product design, and the contrast between the two has shaped

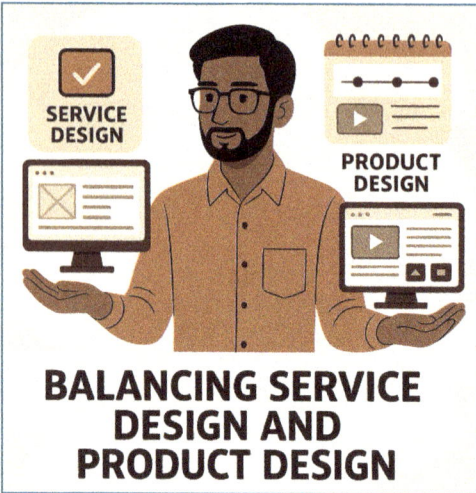

BALANCING SERVICE DESIGN AND PRODUCT DESIGN

how I think about my role as a UX professional.

In the service sector, the pace is relentless. Every month, or sometimes every few weeks, I was handed a new client. One month it might be a gym, the next an interior design firm. Each project required a complete reset of my perspective: a crash course in the client's business model, the pain points of their customers, and the outcomes they cared about most. The timeline was short, the relationship temporary. Our mandate was simple: deliver something tangible, *and* deliver it fast. There was little room for extensive research or long discovery cycles. Agility was the currency of success.

Product design, on the other hand, moves to a different rhythm. The engagement stretches across months, sometimes years. The scope is broader, the stakes higher, and the horizon longer. You are not just solving today's problems, you are aligning with where the business wants to be six months, a year, or even three years down the line. Because of that, the work unfolds in phases: research and discovery, low-fidelity exploration, and high-fidelity design. There is time to test assumptions, iterate, and refine before development begins.

The process often starts with a kickoff meeting. If a client arrives with a clear vision, the team can dive directly into detailed design. More often, though, clarity is missing. Product managers or executives may think they know what they need, but the real work lies in uncovering the gap between assumptions and reality. That is where research becomes essential. We step back, talk to users, test ideas, and build evidence into the process—something rarely possible in service engagements with compressed timelines.

This difference in pacing shapes everything. In short service projects, research is often the first thing sacrificed. The deadlines do not allow for much beyond quick outputs. In product design, research is not just possible, it is vital. It anchors the work in real human needs and ensures the solution will endure over time.

For me, that is the defining contrast. Service design demands agility: the ability to pivot quickly, absorb new contexts, and deliver value under pressure. Product design allows for depth: the patience to explore, test, and evolve an experience until it truly fits. Both are valuable, but they call for entirely different mindsets. Knowing which hat you are wearing, and when, makes all the difference.

The Lesson: No One-Size-Fits-All Approach to UX

Working across both service design and product design taught me that context dictates process. In service-based projects, where timelines are measured in weeks, research often gets squeezed out. The challenge is not a lack of value; it is a lack of time. In those situations, success depends on agility, quick framing, and designing with just enough fidelity to meet client needs.

Product design, on the other hand, lives on a much longer horizon. Here, the luxury and the responsibility is depth. With time to plan in phases, research is not optional; it is essential. A product team that invests in discovery, user testing, and iterative design builds solutions that last.

The contrast made me realize that design is not one-size-fits-all. The tempo, expectations, and deliverables must adapt to the project's scope and business model.

I also learned that flexibility does not mean abandoning principles. Even on short service projects, it is still possible to apply a user-centered mindset by asking sharper questions at kickoff, by framing design options through likely user pain points, or by creating lean prototypes that spark discussion. On the product side, the risk is the opposite: getting bogged down in endless phases without ever delivering. Balance matters everywhere.

Ultimately, the lesson is this: know the rhythms of the environment you are in and adjust your methods accordingly. Agility and depth are both valuable, but neither works in every situation. The best designers learn to switch gears, and to carry the mindset of problem-solving, empathy, and clarity into whichever context they face.

Call to Action: Flex Your Process to Fit the Project

Adapt your approach. Recognize whether you are in a short-term service engagement or a long-term product partnership. Adjust your design methods to fit the time horizon.

Prioritize discovery wisely. For service projects with tight deadlines, focus on rapid stakeholder alignment and lightweight validation. For product work, invest deeply in research and phased design.

Set clear expectations. Communicate to clients what is possible within the project's scope and timeline. If research is not feasible, explain the trade-offs.

Build flexibility into your process. Stay ready to switch gears, from wireframes to high-fidelity design, based on the client's clarity and readiness.

Anchor in the mission. Whether in service or product contexts, keep the ultimate goal front and center: solving real problems and helping customers succeed.

James Young: Internal vs. External Politics
The Politics of Credibility

There's a stark difference between working on an internal UX team and walking in as an outside consultant. Internal teams

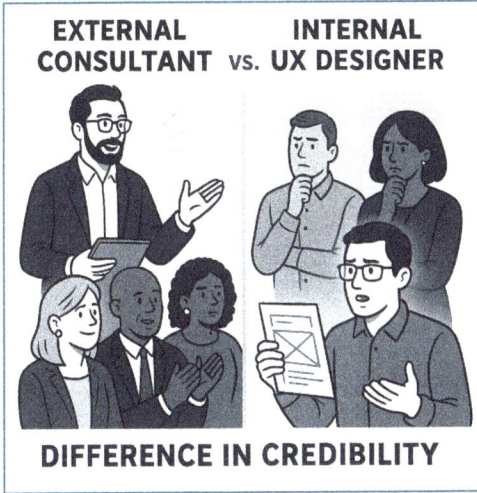

EXTERNAL CONSULTANT vs. **INTERNAL UX DESIGNER**

DIFFERENCE IN CREDIBILITY

wrestle with politics every day. They fight for access to customers, defend design time, and justify their existence in the face of competing priorities. Consultants, on the other hand, often arrive with built-in credibility. By the time leadership admits that something is broken and signs a contract, there is already an openness to change. The consultant becomes the catalyst, pulling executives and stakeholders into conversations that internal teams may have spent years trying, and failing, to initiate.

I tried to recreate that same dynamic as an insider by building what I call "inflection points." These are moments when leadership is forced to pause, reconsider, and sometimes even pivot. Creating them is risky. Done well, they can spark transformation. Done poorly, they can damage trust. I have seen both outcomes. Sometimes all it takes is reframing an old problem in a new light or bringing together product, marketing, technology, and support leaders in a way they have never gathered before. Suddenly, the conversation changes. Other times, those same attempts sour relationships if they are perceived as a challenge to authority.

That is the tightrope of internal politics. Suggest a radical change and you risk insulting the very people who built the legacy systems. Push for customer research and you may be told it is too dangerous to show prototypes to users who already resent the product. Even documenting compromises, so UX is not blamed when poor choices backfire, can feel like overstepping.

Consultants do not carry that burden in the same way. They formalize tradeoffs in contracts and scope documents. Every compromise has a signature. Internal teams, on the other hand, see their decisions dissolve into the noise of delivery pressure, leaving them exposed when results fall short.

That's why I believe in hybrid models. The best organizations embed designers deeply within product teams so they understand the daily reality, while also maintaining a consultative layer with the authority to challenge assumptions at the enterprise level. It is not a matter of choosing one or the other. The real strength comes from balance.

In the end, whether you are inside or outside, the politics never go away. The difference lies in whether the organization treats design as overhead to be squeezed or as the spark that can reignite true transformation.

The Lesson: Navigating Internal vs. External UX Politics

Working as part of an internal UX team and stepping in as an outside consultant may look similar on the surface, but the politics are vastly different. Inside, the challenge is credibility. Internal teams must fight for access, defend their process, and justify design value in environments where legacy systems and entrenched priorities dominate. Outside, credibility is granted from the start because leadership has already admitted something is broken and is ready for change.

The lesson is twofold. First, internal teams need to create their own inflection points. These moments force the organization to pause, regroup, and rethink. Without them, UX risks being sidelined as overhead rather than embraced as strategy. Second, documentation matters. Consultants thrive because they formalize tradeoffs and scope. Internal teams can protect themselves in the same way by capturing compromises, making it clear when shortcuts will weaken outcomes.

Most importantly, politics are not a distraction from UX. They are part of it. Building alliances, framing insights in terms that resonate with leadership, and showing how user-centered practices support business goals are as critical as research or design. Whether you are inside or outside, the real work is influence. The organizations that succeed are those that treat design not as an expense, but as the spark that ignites transformation.

Call to Action: Turning UX Politics into Leverage

Create inflection points. Don't wait for leadership to admit something is broken. Use research, prototypes, or customer stories to spark moments that force the organization to pause and reconsider.

Document compromises. When shortcuts are imposed, write them down. Make it clear what was traded away and what risks were accepted. This protects the UX team from blame later and keeps accountability visible.

Translate insights into business terms. Frame usability problems as revenue risks, efficiency gains, or opportunities for customer loyalty. Speak the language leaders use to make decisions.

Build alliances across functions. UX rarely wins alone. Partner with product managers, engineers, and support staff to present a united case for user-centered improvements.

Adopt a consultant's mindset. Even as an internal team, act with the structure and formality of an outside agency. Prepare kickoff sessions, set expectations, and document outcomes to raise credibility.

Chapter 8: Final Thoughts

It's easy to get caught in the administrivia—running design reviews, answering emails, participating in standups and postmortems, and churning out deliverables to feed the Agile machine. But in the rush to keep up, we sometimes forget the larger mission that brought us to this career in the first place.

UX isn't a job you master and keep repeating on autopilot. The core challenge of UX is dealing with constant change.

We must constantly learn new ways to build UX coalitions if we are to lead our organizations forward.

We must constantly challenge the status quo—not for disruption's sake, but to improve outcomes for users and the business.

And, as my stories and the stories of our colleagues in Chapter 7 have made clear, we must constantly develop more effective ways to navigate the politics of UX.

Without political savvy, our best research and design efforts won't survive the corporate bureaucracy long enough to positively impact the lives of our customers. And positively impacting customers' lives is our true mission.

In this chapter, I share some final thoughts on the state of the profession today and where I think we may go from here.

The State of UX Today
We Aren't There Yet

There was a moment in 2019 when I thought UX had finally arrived. It felt like we had crossed a threshold, as if no serious product could reach the market without thoughtful attention to the user experience. My own team was making great strides: routinely conducting on-site research, simplifying complex applications and aligning them with customer goals, and infusing UX into the corporate culture. For the first time, I began to wonder if the Age of Experience had finally arrived.

I even considered stepping away from in-house roles to move into consulting. Maybe, I thought, the real work of UX was now about fine-tuning mature practices and helping organizations polish systems that already had a solid UX foundation.

And then the pandemic came.

My wife, who was teaching kindergarten at the time, was suddenly thrust into remote instruction. Her school rolled out a brand-new ed-tech platform to support the transition. I was working at home and available to offer tech support when needed. What we experienced with that application completely reset my optimism about UX. The interface was haphazard and the workflows were nonsensical. It had invisible hotspots that navigated to other screens, obviously left over from development. It was obvious that no teacher, or even an attentive human, had been involved in the design process.

For all the progress we had made in advancing UX, there were still vast domains where even the fundamentals were not being applied. My illusion that our work was nearly finished was gone.

I realized again why this field matters so much. If something as critical as education can be derailed by bad design, then our mission is far from complete. UX still has a long way to go, and so do we.

The Lesson: The Practice of UX Isn't Complete

With all the progress we've made over the past several decades, it's tempting to believe that UX has arrived. For a moment, I believed the hardest battles were behind us and the discipline had finally secured its rightful place as an essential business strategy. The reality is more sobering. Even as some industries embrace advanced design practices, others still neglect the fundamentals.

Education, healthcare, government, and other essential sectors still suffer from design that ignores human needs. A single bad experience in these fields can have consequences far more serious than frustration. And with the resurgence of AI tools, the practice of UX design will fundamentally change in ways that we are just now beginning to understand.

Call to Action: Never Stop Asking: "What's Next?"

Question your current methodologies. The practice of UX has become bloated with meaningless methods and activities. One recent book on design thinking described over 100 disconnected tools you can use. Break down your UX practice into activities and evaluate which are helping you understand and redesign the user experience, and which are activities without achievement.

Ensure all your UX activities connect. Many times, UXers perform activities that are ignored as soon as they're completed. Every activity should receive input from its predecessor and produce output for its successor. There should be a continuous flow of data from initial research through deployment.

Adopt an AI-first approach. Use an AI tool to assist your activities. Experimentation is the only way we will understand what AI can and can't do well. Keep an open mind and look for ways that AI can enable you to do things you never had time to do.

The Quest for Simplicity
Detecting When Effort Exceeds Value

Incremental improvements to products and services are a large part of the practice of UX, but we all dream of the opportunity to lead a

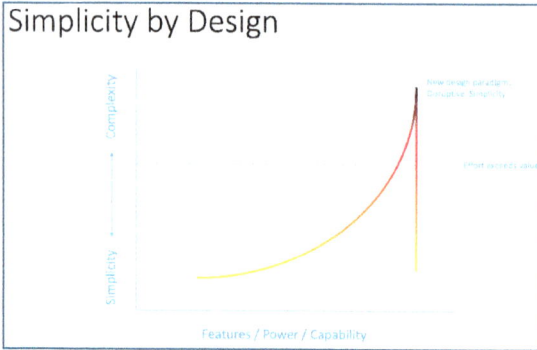

Simplicity by Design

revolutionary redesign, the kind that transforms an experience from overwhelming complexity back to "don't make me think" simplicity.

If you study the history of technology, you'll discover a familiar pattern. A product begins as a lab curiosity, designed by engineers for engineers. It evolves into a complex tool for early adopters, typically hobbyists who enjoy tinkering with new tech. Eventually, it becomes domesticated into a consumer product that almost anyone can use. This evolutionary pathway is still operating today, but often with disruptive consequences to the technology's originator.

In the Age of Agile, when a product first launches, it's usually delivered as a minimal viable product (MVP). Over time, new features are added and functionality grows, but so does operational complexity. The more features you have, the harder it is to find the one you're looking for. And often those new features are implemented in machine-centric terms that make sense to engineers but not to users.

After several releases, the product is both highly capable and highly complex. The original UI framework does not scale to accommodate the weight of every new feature that has been added. At this stage, the *effort* required to use the product often exceeds its perceived *value* in the eyes of customers. If users begin to think that the work required to get results with the product is not worth their time, it opens the door for competitors to enter the market with simpler, more intuitive alternatives.

We've seen this play out before. BlackBerry once dominated the smartphone market, prized for its email and security features. But as functionality grew, so did complexity, and the experience began to feel clunky and constrained. Then the iPhone arrived with a revolutionary redesign that simplified how people interacted with a smartphone. BlackBerry's complexity left it vulnerable, and Apple seized the opportunity.

Organizations often try to solve this problem with incremental fixes like tweaks to navigation and adjustments to labeling that make small usability gains. But once a product tips too far toward complexity, incrementalism is not enough. A revolutionary redesign is required, one that retains all of the product's functionality but radically reduces the complexity of how users access it.

The Lesson: Sometimes Incrementalism Is Not Enough

Incremental "enhancements" are the everyday work of UX, and they are important. But the work every UX professional dreams of is revolutionary redesign when we don't just polish an interface or streamline a workflow but fundamentally reimagine the experience.

Convincing stakeholders that a revolutionary redesign is required is difficult. Business pressures, tight timelines, and organizational inertia keep us operating in the realm of small wins. But when the opportunity comes to step back, cast off the assumptions baked into the current framework, and rebuild from the ground up, the impact is game changing. The result is a product that is just as powerful but dramatically simpler and redefines the market.

Call to Action: Read the Story in Smashing Magazine

Search for my name at smashingmagazine.com. I can't list all the calls to action here. Search for the article I wrote describing one of my revolutionary redesign projects in Smashing Magazine.

Nothing Lasts Forever
Change Is the Only Constant

When I landed my first job at HP in 1982, I thought I would retire there. The culture was strong, the people cared about each other, and leadership genuinely believed in delivering excellent products. There were no layoffs. Shareholders were never mentioned in company meetings; leaders only talked about initiatives to enhance the lives of employees and customers.

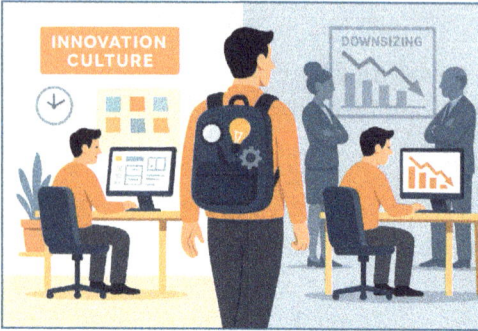

When headhunters called, I ignored them. Most of us did. We were paid fairly, respected, and doing work we loved. Why would anyone leave?

But nothing lasts forever. The economy shifts. Cultures evolve. Leaders come and go. Colleagues you relied on move elsewhere. Sometimes these changes elevate the organization, but at other times they completely change the company's values and work environment.

I've worked at companies where UX maturity rose to impressive levels, only to watch it unravel when new leadership arrived. I have felt secure one year, only to face a layoff the next. I have watched the UX profession rise into one of the most sought-after disciplines, then contract as markets shifted and technologies like AI redefined the practice.

No situation is permanent. Whether you are in a thriving culture or a toxic one, change will come. The question is how you will respond. You need to sharpen your perception for spotting change on the horizon and have a strategy in place, whether that means learning new skills, adapting your role, or finding a new place to do your best work.

One thing, however, never changes: the enduring value of people who can empathize with others, who see problems no one else can see, and who have the creative drive to craft innovative solutions. These are personal attributes you can carry anywhere. Cultivate them. Be proud of them. Because no matter how much things change in our profession, the human-centered mindset will always be needed.

The Lesson: Change Agents Versus Change Victims

Regardless of how comfortable or secure you feel in your role, things can change quickly. Company culture, leadership priorities, or the economy can all shift in ways that make yesterday's dream job today's nightmare.

What never changes, however, is the value of empathy, creativity, and the ability to spot problems others miss. These traits make UX professionals resilient, even as markets and technologies evolve. The key is to recognize that while your environment may shift, your ways of seeing and responding to the world remain a durable advantage. The best way to protect yourself from change is to drive it.

Call to Action: Constantly Assess Your Career Trajectory

Stay alert to signs of change. Don't ignore early signals of shifting priorities, leadership styles, or declining culture. Recognizing these trends early gives you more options.

Always have a strategy. Whether it is updating your skills, strengthening your professional network, or quietly preparing for a job search, plan for change before you are forced into it.

Invest in adaptability. Learn new tools, explore emerging practices, and position yourself as someone who can pivot quickly when the market, technology, or company shifts.

Protect your passion. Don't let toxic environments drain your sense of purpose. If you need to move on to preserve your professional joy, do it.

Where Do We Go from Here?
The Future of Our Profession

AI is rapidly shifting the landscape of UX, automating tasks that once consumed days or weeks and compressing them into seconds. Wireframes, flows, and even polished visuals can now be generated almost instantly. This means the value of UX no longer lies in production alone. The real work, the enduring work, is rooted in human insight: interpreting customer needs and understanding how products shape and fit into people's lives.

This raises a sobering question: what's left for UX when AI does the production work? Perhaps the better question is not only what's left for UX, but how we can turn what remains into work that organizations value and will invest in.

The danger right now is that many executives overestimate AI's ability to replicate the responsibilities of human researchers and designers. They don't understand the depth of our expertise; they only see our surface-level deliverables. This is why they believe UX professionals can be replaced by AI.

But I believe that, in the coming months, organizations that cut UX teams in favor of AI will discover that quality and competitiveness suffer. When that happens, UX professionals will be welcomed back but now equipped with more powerful tools. The practice of UX will evolve, but the change will strengthen those who embrace AI to amplify and expedite their contributions.

AI makes tight deadlines for big problems more manageable. UX strike teams now have AI tools to experiment rapidly and discard or merge concepts until the team converges on a solution.

While AI can accelerate UX activities, it is incapable of *"Aha!"* moments or genuine empathy for users. It can draft mockups in seconds, but only under the guidance of someone who understands users, context, and design. From what I've seen so far, AI tools are great at producing a first draft of research insights, data analysis, and experience designs, but like all first drafts, more iteration is required before a final solution is reached, and that iteration can only be performed by, or under the direction of, human beings.

While others may not recognize it, the value of UX and product design has never been constrained to wireframes or design artifacts. The true value lies in our ability to analyze and streamline the invisible conversation between people and products. We identify hidden problems in the user–product system and reimagine solutions that others may not see. Prototypes and mockups are only the vehicles for expressing those solutions.

Nevertheless, we are left with existential questions, and we must be prepared for hard answers.

Our goal, our mission, is to provide the people who use our products with the best possible experience en route to the outcomes they want to achieve. So:

- If, in the future, AI can achieve our mission when given the right inputs, will the practice of UX then be fully automated?
- Will design be reduced to inputting the context and specs and then asking an AI tool to output the experience?
- Will the future of UX be reduced to creating an inventory of intents?
- Can AI, on its own, create the architecture of an intent-driven application, design it, test it, and code it?
- Or will UX become more about revolutionary redesign, delegating incremental enhancements to AI?

For UX leaders, the redefinition of our profession has always been on the horizon but is now unavoidable. The craft must go deeper. Deliverables may get faster, but strategy, analysis, and sense-making are the skills that set human practitioners apart. They are also the parts of the discipline that often resist neat measurement and tidy ROI metrics, which means they require persistence and advocacy to sustain.

Finally, we must become skilled in championing the difference between *out*puts and *out*comes—to shift the company's focus from *building products* to *delivering results*.

The Lesson: UX Is at an Inflection Point

In the past, UX was exciting because it was an ever-evolving discipline. New methods and principles were being discovered all the time. In today's Agile world, UX has become almost thoughtless, routine, and mechanical—a design factory whose output even AI can simulate.

My hope is that the near future awakens a UX renaissance. A rebirth of the *mission* of UX taking precedence over the *job* of UX, an exploration of the first principles and governing dynamics of human-technology communication and collaboration. There will be no immediate payoff for this endeavor, but the long-term benefits will be immeasurable.

Call to Action: Don't Protect the Past; Embrace the Future

Run an experiment. Go through the activities you perform over the course of a project, from research, to analysis, to design iterations, to feeding the Agile machine. Begin each activity by employing an AI tool to see what it can and cannot do. Evaluate its usefulness, accuracy, and quality. When is it helpful? When is it not? What work is left to be done after AI has made its attempt?

Look for unanswered questions. For example, ChatGPT can perform sentiment analysis instantly. But what questions are left that need answering? If the analysis indicates your customers rate your company poorly, *why* do they rate it this way? What additional research is needed to understand the "why?"

Redefine your role. Stop measuring your value in terms of wireframes or screens. Measure it in outcomes, specifically how well the product helps people achieve meaningful results. Focus your presentations, deliverables, and metrics on this mission.

Show the before and after. When conducting design reviews, show the starting point that AI generated and compare it to the final deliverable that you refined drawing on your UX expertise.

Update your resumé. Don't just say I use AI. For each UX skill, indicate *how* you use AI as a partner to maximize your productivity. Quantify the increase in productivity that AI tools have made possible compared to your previous projects.

Educate leadership. Help your executives see AI for what it is: a powerful partner in production, but not a substitute for design vision. Show them how combining human judgment with machine efficiency produces the best results for your users and your company.

Shift your focus from outputs to outcomes. Don't define your value by the number of wireframes or screens you produce. Define it by the human impact your work enables.

Protect time for inquiry. Advocate for space outside the sprint cycle to explore deeper questions about users, systems, and contexts. Carve out time for reflection, not just production.

Develop AI fluency. Take courses, watch tutorials, and experiment with AI tools in your everyday work. Learn their strengths and limitations.

Treat AI like a junior colleague. Imagine that AI is an intern. Remember all that tedious work you do that takes so much time? Give it to AI. Guide and refine its outputs while staying accountable for quality. Liberate yourself to focus on the deep work you love to do and let AI do the routine jobs.

Share what you've learned. As you navigate through this period, share your discoveries with the rest of us. Speak at conferences. Write books. Post on LinkedIn. Help us understand what works and what doesn't. As the thought leaders of tomorrow, we need to hear from you.

About the Author

For more than forty years, I've lived and worked inside the evolving world of user experience as a researcher, designer, engineer, teacher, and manager. I've spent my career helping teams turn human insight into better products while navigating the complex politics that often stand in the way of great design.

I've led UX and content design groups inside Fortune 50 corporations, global consultancies, and small technology firms, building solutions for consumers, businesses, employees, and even children. Along the way, I've learned that the hardest part of design isn't crafting the user experience—it's the people, the culture, and the systems that often get in your way.

Today, I continue to explore better ways to foster communication and collaboration between products and the people who use them. My mission is to reduce the cognitive and emotional burdens that technology places on us, and to help organizations rediscover what's possible when they place the human first.

www.ingramcontent.com/pod-product-compliance
Lightning Source LLC
Chambersburg PA
CBHW071648200326
41519CB00012BA/2438